ESSAYS ON REFERENCE, LANGUAGE, AND MIND

ESSAYS ON REFERENCE, LANGUAGE, AND MIND

Keith Donnellan

Edited by Joseph Almog

AND

Paolo Leonardi

OXFORD
UNIVERSITY PRESS

Oxford University Press, Inc., publishes works that further
Oxford University's objective of excellence
in research, scholarship, and education.

Oxford New York
Auckland Cape Town Dar es Salaam Hong Kong Karachi
Kuala Lumpur Madrid Melbourne Mexico City Nairobi
New Delhi Shanghai Taipei Toronto

With offices in
Argentina Austria Brazil Chile Czech Republic France Greece
Guatemala Hungary Italy Japan Poland Portugal Singapore
South Korea Switzerland Thailand Turkey Ukraine Vietnam

Published by Oxford University Press, Inc.
198 Madison Avenue, New York, New York 10016

www.oup.com

Library of Congress Cataloging-in-Publication Data
Donnellan, Keith.
Essays on reference, language, and mind / Keith Donnellan ; edited by
Joseph Almog and Paolo Leonardi.
p. cm.
ISBN 978-0-19-985799-9 (alk. paper)
1. Philosophy, American—20th century. 2. Philosophy,
American—21st century. 3. Reference (Philosophy) 4. Language
and languages—Philosophy. 5. Philosophy of mind. I. Almog, Joseph.
II. Leonardi, Paolo. III. Title.
B945.D6251A46 2012
121'.68—dc23 2012003947

1 3 5 7 9 8 6 4 2
Printed in the United States of America
on acid-free paper

CONTENTS

EDITOR'S PREFACE:

Keith Donnellan—Philosophy by Ear

A few months ago, after fifteen years of retirement in northern California, surrounded by fine horses, quality wines, and English detective novels, Keith Donnellan showed up one Thursday afternoon in the old room of the philosophy of language workshop, which he did so much to launch in the late eighties.[1] He listened patiently to a series of celebratory speeches. But if you tracked his body language, he seemed like an athlete in the starting blocks waiting for the sprint to start. When it did, four cutting-edge papers, all commenting on his work, were given by quick-witted young philosophers. A heated discussion ensued each time, led by the tribe's leaders, David Kaplan and Tyler Burge. Four papers led to four hours of high-speed sparring. And four times over, this unassuming and shy man made a one-paragraph contribution. Fifteen years out of practice, literally out of the woodwork, his comments were always the simplest, the sharpest, and, of course, the most intuitive of all. And though he did not use like the rest of us the high-tech gadgets of "rigid designators," "scope distinctions," and "singular propositions," he spellbound everybody—old hands who knew him well, new grads who never saw him before. A sort of Gandalf the white, a sage from a different era, when direct and intuitive philosophy was still possible, indeed a form of daily life.

My own first realization that Keith Donnellan was endowed with special powers was twenty-four years before that Thursday, when he managed to make me enjoy eating a fish. By then, in my late twenties, I had reneged on all my principles of youth. But not this one last gut feeling—I hated fish. It is my belief that Keith knew I'd never ever eat fish. One day, he invited me to dinner at his place. He was the cook. I was so involved in the conversation that I did not attend at first to what I was eating. Slowly, it grew on me that I was munching on something extraordinarily tasty and that this would be my most memorable culinary experience since childhood days in France. I went on and on celebrating the ingenuity of the food and the cook, not knowing what I was talking about—a *fish*—but referring to it anyway, a vindication of the theoretical views of the cook. As we were about to go home, at the doorway, Keith took me aside and whispered in my ear, "By the way, the thing you kept drooling over the whole evening was a special 'gig' of mine... stuffed fish." There he left the matter, with his little shy and subtle smile. Such was Keith's *sotto voce* style in human interactions, and such was his way in philosophy.

Donnellan did *see* things directly. It was no accident that of all the innovative minds who came to us with game-changing ideas in the late sixties and early seventies, it was Donnellan who came up with the fundamental idea of a *referential* use of a piece of language.

This transformative idea emanates directly from *perceptual* cases. You and I are standing in the alcohol-free party. The man in front of us, Sir Alfred, is holding a martini glass, drinking from it plain water and allowing his tongue to roll. Unbeknownst to us there is only one martini drinker in the party, Bertrand, hidden in the kitchen, where he abuses discreetly of the forbidden juice. Deprived of a rude use of a pointing finger, I say to you in a whisper, "The man drinking a martini is tipsy." Did I say something *true*? Did I say something *of* Sir Alfred? Did I *refer* to Sir Alfred? Thus was engendered the idea of a *referential use*.

The idea came to Donnellan in 1964. But it was published in *Philosophical Review,* in a now classic paper called "Reference and Definite Descriptions," only in 1966. The paper, submitted to PR, was initially... rejected by an external referee. (Keith was at Cornell at the time, so an outside hand was called upon.) It was only the intervention of an internal knowing hand that saved the paper from the absurdities of professional refereeing. And so with a little help from discerning friends, the paper was out in 1966.

Like the negative referee, not everybody was immediately appreciative. These were heady times in the philosophy of language and mind, and the air was filled with ideas that struck a much louder chord.

In the late sixties and all the way to the critical year 1970, the philosophy of language and the philosophy of mind went through related paradigm shifts. The then-reigning paradigm, Frege's theory of language and thought, became the focus of a fundamental critique. A new theory, *direct reference* theory, emerged from the critique. It went on to become the new paradigm, and it is the one informing our perspective today.

The current volume of Donnellan's essays offers a unique two-tiered insight into this 1966–1970 turn. First, we get a new perspective on the distinct contribution of one of the main game changers, Keith Donnellan. Second, and more generally, we are offered a new—somewhat surprising—picture of what "the direct reference turn" was all about.

Keith Donnellan's work in the essays here focuses mainly on (i) the relation of *semantic reference* (and keep in mind the modifying adjective I just used to qualify "reference"), a touchstone notion in the philosophy of language, and (ii) the relation of *thinking about*, of primal concern in the philosophy of mind. I believe that it is fair to say that, until recently, it was commonplace to view Donnellan's work on these two major fronts as significant but, in the end, playing a merely supportive role in the path-breaking changes of 1966–1970. Some held the view of the reluctant referee. But even those who saw the light thought referential uses are a minor sideshow compared with the central stage ideas of "direct reference" and/or "rigid designation."

The current book of classical essays *by* Keith and a companion book of essays *about* Keith may help us form a deeper sense of the various (nonequivalent) innovations offered in 1966 through 1970 and, in particular, to appreciate the very distinct set of foundational ideas proposed by Keith.[2]

So much concerns theoretical matters, the theory of thinking about things and semantically referring to them. But over and above the theoretical issues, there remains the human imprint of this perceptive and innovative thinker. The landscape of the philosophy of logic and language is filled with glamorously brilliant thinkers whose writing style reflects their scintillating minds. One only has to think of Russell, Quine, and Keith's own peers in the 1966–1970 direct reference turn, Kripke, Kaplan, and Putnam. As a person and teacher, Keith shone in his own distinct subtle way. Those who knew him by acquaintance will realize the man's style is reflected in his crystalline papers. Those who will be having him in mind only by way of his papers will come, upon a close rereading the papers, to share this image of a naturally born philosopher.

NOTES

1. The publication of the present volume of essays by Keith Donnellan is accompanied by the publication of a companion volume of essays about Donnellan's work (*With Donnellan in Mind,* OUP, 2012). The companion volume resulted from two recent conferences about his work, in Bologna in March 2008 and at UCLA in May 2008. The present introduction is focused solely on Donnellan's own essays. I owe thanks to comments of T. Burge, B. Herman, S. Shiffrin, J. Carriero, D. Kaplan, T. Martin, S. Cumming, H. Wettstein, S. Coolidge, and my coeditor, P. Leonardi. Earlier on, in Bologna, I benefited from remarks of H. Kamp and J. Perry (for more personal remarks about Keith's philosophical style, see Perry's contribution in the companion volume). Special thanks regarding our understanding of referential uses are due to D. Kaplan. My debt to Keith Donnellan, philosophical and personal, is unique. He is the man who made me understand what is the source of something I lived by—*direct reference*. I am also very grateful to his comments on the present introduction.
2. See fn. 1.

INTRODUCTION

by Keith Donnellan

Collected here are several of my papers on topics in the theory of reference. A theory of reference, as it is to be found in my work, would explain how something becomes the referent of an expression in an utterance by a speaker on a particular occasion or becomes the thing a speaker refers to by using an expression on an occasion. The "thing" here may be a person, an object, a place, or one of the many diverse sorts of things we talk about—a play, a political movement, a theory of structure of the atom, to mention only a few. Some of these may in the end require special treatment in their own right.

Several of these papers can be seen as attempting to accomplish two aims. First, I try to refute a standard reply to the question, "What determines the referent, if there is one, of definite descriptions and proper names?" I will call it the "identifying descriptions view," following my use in the paper "Proper Names and Identifying Descriptions."* Second, an answer to this same question is sketched out or

* I believe that the paper "Proper Names and Identifying Descriptions" (1970) is the earliest publication of the argument it presents for the conclusion that the referents of proper names are not established through associated descriptions.

used in several papers. Simply put, I argue that in a wide range of cases of the use of these two important kinds of singular terms, it is not a set of descriptions that determines the referent, but rather the intention of the speaker in using the term. The identifying descriptions view, in contrast, would hold that if definite descriptions, for example, have referents, then the descriptive content of the description will provide the referent; it will be that which satisfied the description uniquely. To obtain uniqueness, the uttered description will perhaps require augmentation by certain unexpressed descriptions from the content of utterance (for example, if the overt description is "the man drinking a martini," it may need to be augmented by the unexpressed description "in this room"). The most common version of the identifying descriptions view in regard to proper names appeals to the descriptions that the speaker would or could give as identifying the referent (for example, having used the name "Thales," the speaker might describe the referent as "the ancient Greek philosopher who held that all is water and who fell in a well while contemplating the stars").

As against the identifying descriptions view in each of the mentioned cases, the argument I give in the two main papers on the subject ("Reference and Definite Descriptions" and "Proper Names and Identifying Descriptions") work by way of a variety of constructed examples in which there are different sorts of failures of the descriptions to describe the actual referent. Either the descriptions pick out something that is surely not being referred to, fail to pick out the referent uniquely, or are insufficient to pick out anything at all. And thus the descriptions are not what yield the solution to the problem of how the referent is determined. So, having, as I thought, countered this plausible but wrong view, I went on to adumbrate what I took to be the most promising alternative. Looking at the paper on reference and definite descriptions, I must confess that only one of the two writers mentioned there as my targets, Bertrand Russell and Peter Strawson, could fairly be said to have held that definite descriptions are used to refer and that the entity referred to is identified in virtue of its having the properties mentioned in the description (plus properties assumed from the context of utterance). Of the two it is Peter Strawson who, in his (at the time of my paper's publication) widely read paper, "On Referring", espouses this view. He says, for example:

> In the case of phrases of the form 'the so-and-so' used referringly, use of 'the' together with the position of the phrase in the sentence . . . acts as a signal that a unique reference is being made and the following noun, or noun and adjective, together with the context of utterance, shows what unique reference is being made.[1]

Strawson, then, is an example of one who holds an identifying descriptions view about definite descriptions. This, however, is not true of the second target of the paper, Bertrand Russell. He needed nothing to determine the referent of any use of a definite description, for definite descriptions on his view do not refer at all, and hence there is nothing to identify. Only what he calls 'genuine' or 'logically' proper names can perform reference. And the rarefied requirements for using these is such that they cannot even occur in ordinary discourse. And to utterances in ordinary discourse containing definite descriptions Russell would apply, of course, his well-known theory, which shows them to be composed of a conjunction of quantified sentences, the definite description having disappeared. As against Russell, I wanted to show that while there are many uses of definite descriptions, what I called "attributive" uses, to which I was (and am) happy to apply Russell's analysis, there is also an equally large, important, and quite normal use of them in which they do refer. These,

I called, (what else?) "referential" uses. The constructed examples mentioned were meant to be of this latter sort.

The papers "Reference and Definite Descriptions" and "Proper Names and Identifying Descriptions" were chronologically my first papers on the subject of reference (1964 and 1970) and also express the theoretical basis for my further forays into the topic. I would like here to add a few comments to these two base papers.

I should have supplemented the paper on definite descriptions, I now believe, by pointing to some features of the situations involving referential definite descriptions that give reason to think that the sentence uttered cannot be analyzed via Russell's theory of descriptions, features other than the fact that the speaker seems to be making a reference in uttering the sentence. This would have blocked any suggestion that while the sentence uttered may be analyzed as Russell proposes, some other feature of the situation gives rise to our intuition that reference is going on.[2] Here I will point to two such characteristics that seem to argue against treating the sentence according to Russell's theory.

The first characteristic of the situations is that very many of them involve what I have called "indefinite definite descriptions." Howard Wettstein[3] has shown, I believe, that this fact raises a problem for the treatment of the uttered sentences according to Russell's theory, a problem that cannot be removed by the usual maneuver of augmenting the description by features from the context. It is, he also maintains, no problem for the position of my paper that referential definite descriptions are on a par with names and demonstratives as making direct reference rather than introducing a quantified form. Let me illustrate what I take to be Wettstein's point with an example or two.

For simplicity, I will restrict myself to simple sentences of the form 'The Φ is Ψ,' and I will hope it is agreed that if an uttered sentence on an occasion is correctly analyzable, say, as in Russell's theory of descriptions, then the speaker on that occasion can be held to have asserted the proposition such an analysis implies. At a largish college party, suppose a speaker has been asked by a visitor whether the dean of the college is present, for the visitor has a need to meet him. The speaker, looking around, sees the dean in the crowd and now is faced with how to bring about a reference to the person he thinks to be the dean. In many circumstances, at least three ways may present themselves. If he knows the name of that person, George Smith, perhaps, and has reason to think the visitor also knows the person by that name, he may choose to use it. If the person he picks out as being the dean is not too far distant, he may point or use some other gesture and a demonstrative: "That is the dean of the college." Or he may describe the person, choosing a description that, if possible, will allow the visitor to correctly pick out the person he intends. And here, or so my view has it, he will very frequently embed the description he comes up with in the linguistic form we call a "definite description." Now, a question arises here: Must the speaker aim at so describing his intended referent as to apply to it uniquely? Well, if we look at practice, it will seem hardly so: Where did I leave my purse? I think the purse is in the car.

There are I don't know how many cars in the world. Yet this might be a satisfactory answer to someone's question. At a large faculty celebratory gathering, a visitor to the college asks, "Who is the dean? I need to introduce myself to him." The speaker, glancing around, replies, "The man drinking a martini is the dean." Is the description to be delimited so as to secure uniqueness by something in the context that the speaker relies on to be understood by the questioner? Well, what is it, and did the speaker think of it or assume it? Most often, cases of what I would see as referential definite descriptions are quite indefinite in this matter and, if simply accepted as such, would give a reason to say that Russell's analysis does not fit here, for on his analysis there is a uniqueness condition. And in order to save his view, many have suggested that augmenting descriptions are assumed by the speaker to be supplied by context. But usually there are, it seems, many possibilities given that could be seen as given by the context. In the last example, shall we say that the augmenting description is "in this room"? But then, what about that man sipping a martini across the room, who isn't the dean or thought to be by the speaker? It is not unlikely that the speaker either didn't notice him or simply ignores him. Perhaps the augmenting description might be "in front of us." But how wide a sweep and how far? Can we say that at the time of utterance the context specifies one possibility rather than all the others? If we cannot, there is not one Russellian analysis to assign to the utterance but rather several.

Suppose we ask, if Russell's analysis will not work in these cases, why do we use the form we call a "definite description." My suggestion is that it might seem natural because there is one and only one thing in these cases of referential definite descriptions that the speaker intends to refer to; it signals that the description is supposed to refer to one definite thing, even when it is not the only thing satisfying the description in the context. Let's go back to my somewhat artificial elucidation of the problem facing the speaker faced with several possible ways of getting his reference across to the audience, who chooses to describe the object of the intended reference. A partial description, which may be all he has resources to give, is very likely to do the job of getting the listener in a position to find the referent. The speaker simply relies on the listener to exercise common sense: "The drinks are on the table in the kitchen." The guest goes into the kitchen. There are, in fact, three tables in the kitchen. One is too small to contain drinks; another, large enough, is covered with the makings of the dinner they will enjoy later; and, lo and behold, there is a table, not a salient table, but it holds an assortment of snacks and drinks. He has no problems with which table the speaker was referring to. The use of description "table," however, was useful, perhaps, in preventing him from looking in the refrigerator or searching cupboards. So I think Wettstein was correct: Indefinite definite descriptions provide reason to doubt the application of Russell's analysis to referential uses, and my treatment of the cases yields a somewhat satisfactory solution to the problem such descriptions may seem to present.

Were what I would call instances of the "referential" use of definite descriptions to be analyzed in accord with Russell's theory, the speaker could be taken as asserting the proposition the theory yields. And the truth conditions of that proposition will depend on the properties of the denotation of the description, if there is one. The denotation should then be treated by speaker and listener as very important. But in fact it seems often that if the description is what I count as referential, the denotation is treated as irrelevant. So if the speaker says, "The man drinking a martini is the dean" in our example, and it turns out that the man he intended to refer to has only water in a martini glass, the truth or falsity of the utterance is still a matter of whether that man is the dean. Finding another man who is drinking a martini, but not the intended reference, will not make the utterance true if he turns out to be the dean nor make it false if he is not, even if that man is the sole drinker of a martini. Thus another feature we would expect to hold if a Russellian proposition is involved fails to be present.

The main thing I wish to say about the third of the essays reprinted here, "Proper Names and Identifying Descriptions," is that it was for me a natural extension of the views on definite descriptions. Here the descriptions involved are those supposedly internal and available to a user of a proper name. On the view I attack, it is these that determine or identify the referent. This explanation of how the referent of a proper name is determined was, I think, both widespread and not at all unintuitive. The structure of the argument in this paper paralleled that in the previous paper on referential definite descriptions: By several constructed examples, I hoped to show that the referent of a proper name used on a particular occasion could be identified, even though the descriptions available to the speaker were mainly false of that referent, not uniquely identifying or identifying of the wrong thing. The way in which the referent comes to be known, in each of these examples in the paper, was by finding reason or evidence of the intentions of the speaker in using the name; to what did he or she intend to refer? And the reason or evidence is not restricted to the descriptions of the referent possibly given by the speaker, although such descriptions, if available, may give reason or evidence for concluding that this or that is the referent. The positive thesis of the paper was the same as the previous one also: The speaker's intentions provide the ultimate answer.

I would like to express my gratitude to the editors, Joseph Almog and Paolo Leonardi, for suggesting this collection, for selecting the papers, and for seeing to its publication. Without their interest and labor, it would not exist to be denoted or referred to.

NOTES

1. "On Referring," in Anthony Flew, ed., *Essays in Conceptual Analysis*, London, Macmillan, 1956, pp. 21–52. The quote is from p. 45.
2. See for such a conclusion: Saul Kripke, "Speaker's Reference and Semantic Reference," *Midwest Studies in Philosophy* 2, pp. 255–276. This is not the place to investigate Kripke's somewhat complex apparatus and argument. Of course, if sufficient reasons for denying that a speaker's sentence employing, in my sense, a 'referential definite description' is to be analyzed via Russell's theory, that would be to refute Kripke's conclusion.
3. "Demonstrative Reference and Definite Descriptions," *Philosophical Studies*, 40, pp. 241–257.

ESSAYS ON REFERENCE

[1]

REFERENCE AND DEFINITE DESCRIPTIONS

I

Definite descriptions, I shall argue, have two possible functions.[1] They are used to refer to what a speaker wishes to talk about, but they are also used quite differently. Moreover, a definite description occurring in one and the same sentence may, on different occasions of its use, function in either way. The failure to deal with this duality of function obscures the genuine referring use of definite descriptions. The best-known theories of definite descriptions, those of Russell and Strawson, I shall suggest, are both guilty of this. Before discussing this distinction in use, I will mention some features of these theories to which it is especially relevant.

On Russell's view a definite description may denote an entity: "if '*C*' is a denoting phrase [as definite descriptions are by definition], it may happen that there is one entity *x* (there cannot be more than one) for which the proposition '*x* is identical with *C*' is true.... We may then say that the entity *x* is the denotation of the

First published in *The Philosophical Review*, 1966, **75**: 281–304)

phrase '*C*.' "[2] In using a definite description, then, a speaker may use an expression which denotes some entity, but this is the only relationship between that entity and the use of the definite description recognized by Russell. I shall argue, however, that there are two uses of definite descriptions. The definition of denotation given by Russell is applicable to both, but in one of these the definite description serves to do something more. I shall say that in this use the speaker uses the definite description to *refer* to something, and call this use the "referential use" of a definite description. Thus, if I am right, referring is not the same as denoting and the referential use of definite descriptions is not recognized on Russell's view.

Furthermore, on Russell's view the type of expression that comes closest to performing the function of the referential use of definite descriptions turns out, as one might suspect, to be a proper name (in "the narrow logical sense"). Many of the things said about proper names by Russell can, I think, be said about the referential use of definite descriptions without straining senses unduly. Thus the gulf Russell thought he saw between names and definite descriptions is narrower than he thought.

Strawson, on the other hand, certainly does recognize a referential use of definite definitions. But what I think he did not see is that a definite description may have a quite different role—may be used nonreferentially, even as it occurs in one and the same sentence. Strawson, it is true, points out nonreferential uses of definite descriptions,[3] but which use a definite description has seems to be for him a function of the kind of sentence in which it occurs; whereas, if I am right, there can be two possible uses of a definite description in the same sentence. Thus, in "On Referring," he says, speaking of expressions used to refer, "Any expression of any of these classes [one being that of definite descriptions] can occur as the subject of what would traditionally be regarded as a singular subject-predicate sentence;

and would, so occurring, exemplify the use I wish to discuss."[4] So the definite description in, say, the sentence "The Republican candidate for president in 1968 will be a conservative" presumably exemplifies the referential use. But if I am right, we could not say this of the sentence in isolation from some particular occasion on which it is used to state something; and then it might or might not turn out that the definite description has a referential use.

Strawson and Russell seem to me to make a common assumption here about the question of how definite descriptions function: that we can ask how a definite description functions in some sentence independently of a particular occasion upon which it is used. This assumption is not really rejected in Strawson's arguments against Russell. Although he can sum up his position by saying, " 'Mentioning' or 'referring' is not something an expression does; it is something that someone can use an expression to do,"[5] he means by this to deny the radical view that a "genuine" referring expression *has* a referent, functions to refer, independent of the context of some use of the expression. The denial of this view, however, does not entail that definite descriptions cannot be identified as referring expressions in a sentence unless the sentence is being used. Just as we can speak of a function of a tool that is not at the moment performing its function, Strawson's view, I believe, allows us to speak of the referential function of a definite description in a sentence even when it is not being used. This, I hope to show, is a mistake.

A second assumption shared by Russell's and Strawson's account of definite descriptions is this. In many cases a person who uses a definite description can be said (in some sense) to presuppose or imply that something fits the description.[6] If I state that the king is on his throne, I presuppose or imply that there is a king. (At any rate, this would be a natural thing to say for anyone who doubted that there is a king.) Both Russell and Strawson assume that where the presupposition or implication is false, the truth value of what the speaker says is affected. For Russell the statement made is false; for Strawson it has no truth value. Now if there are two uses of definite descriptions, it may be that the truth value is affected differently in each case by the falsity of the presupposition or implication. This is what I shall in fact argue. It will turn out, I believe, that one or the other of the two views, Russell's or Strawson's, may be correct about the nonreferential use of definite descriptions, but neither fits the referential use. This is not so surprising about Russell's view, since he did not recognize this use in any case, but it is surprising about Strawson's since the referential use is what he tries to explain and defend. Furthermore, on Strawson's account, the result of there being nothing which fits the description is a failure of reference.[7] This too, I believe, turns out not to be true about the referential use of definite descriptions.

II

There are some uses of definite descriptions which carry neither any hint of a referential use nor any presupposition or implication that something fits the description. In general, it seems, these are recognizable from the sentence frame in which the description occurs. These uses will not interest us, but it is necessary to point them out if only to set them aside.

An obvious example would be the sentence "The present king of France does not exist," used, say, to correct someone's mistaken impression that de Gaulle is the king of France.

A more interesting example is this. Suppose someone were to ask, "Is de Gaulle the king of France?" This is the natural form of words for a person to use who is in doubt as to whether de Gaulle is king or president of France. Given this background to the question, there seems to be no presupposition or implication that someone is the king of France. Nor is the person attempting to refer to someone by using the definite description. On the other hand, reverse the name and description in the question and the speaker probably would be thought to presuppose or imply this. "Is the king of France de Gaulle?" is the natural question for one to ask who wonders whether it is de Gaulle rather than someone else who occupies the throne of France.[8]

Many times, however, the use of a definite description does carry a presupposition or implication that something fits the description. If definite descriptions do have a referring role, it will be here. But it is a mistake, I think, to try, as I believe both Russell and Strawson do, to settle this matter without further ado. What is needed, I believe, is the distinction I will now discuss.

III

I will call the two uses of definite descriptions I have in mind the attributive use and the referential use. A speaker who uses a definite description attributively in an assertion states something about whoever or whatever is the so-and-so. A speaker who uses a definite description referentially in an assertion, on the other hand, uses the description to enable his audience to pick out whom or what he is talking about and states something about that person or thing. In the first case the definite description might be said to occur essentially, for the speaker wishes to assert something about whatever or whoever fits that description; but in the referential use the definite description is merely one tool for doing a certain job—calling attention to a person or thing—and in general any other device for doing the same job, another description or a name, would do as well. In the attributive use, the attribute of being the so-and-so is all important, while it is not in the referential use.

To illustrate this distinction, in the case of a single sentence, consider the sentence, "Smith's murderer is insane." Suppose first that we come upon poor Smith foully murdered. From the brutal manner of the killing and the fact that Smith was the most lovable person in the world, we might exclaim, "Smith's murderer is insane." I will assume, to make it a simpler case, that in a quite ordinary sense we do not know who murdered Smith (though this is not in the end essential to the case). This, I shall say, is an attributive use of the definite description.

The contrast with such a use of the sentence is one of those situations in which we expect and intend our audience to realize whom we have in mind when we speak of Smith's murderer and, most importantly, to know that it is this person about whom we are going to say something.

For example, suppose that Jones has been charged with Smith's murder and has been placed on trial. Imagine that there is a discussion of Jones's odd behavior at his trial. We might sum up our impression of his behavior by saying, "Smith's murderer is insane." If someone asks to whom we are referring, by using this description, the answer here is "Jones." This, I shall say, is a referential use of the definite description.

That these two uses of the definite description in the same sentence are really quite different can perhaps best be brought out by considering the consequences of the assumption that Smith had no murderer (for example, he in fact committed suicide). In both situations, in using the definite description "Smith's murderer," the speaker in some sense presupposes or implies that there is a murderer. But when we hypothesize that the presupposition or implication is false, there are different results for the two uses. In both cases we have used the predicate "is insane," but in the first case, if there is no murderer, there is no person of whom it could be correctly said that we attributed insanity to him. Such a person could be identified (correctly) only in case someone fitted the description used. But in the second case, where the definite description is simply a means of identifying the person we want to talk about, it is quite possible for the correct identification to be made even though no one fits the description we used.[9] We were speaking about Jones even though he is not in fact Smith's murderer and, in the circumstances imagined, it was his behavior we were commenting upon. Jones might, for example, accuse us of saying false things of him in calling him insane and it would be no defense, I should think, that our description, "the murderer of Smith," failed to fit him.

It is, moreover, perfectly possible for our audience to know to whom we refer, in the second situation, even though they do not share our presupposition. A person hearing our comment in the context imagined might know we are talking about Jones even though he does not think Jones guilty.

Generalizing from this case, we can say, I think, that there are two uses of sentences of the form, "The ϕ is ψ." In the first, if nothing is the ϕ then nothing has been said to be ψ. In the second, the fact that nothing is the ϕ does not have this consequence.

With suitable changes the same difference in use can be formulated for uses of language other than assertions. Suppose one is at a party and, seeing an interesting-looking person holding a martini glass, one asks, "Who is the man drinking a martini?" If it should turn out that there is only water in the glass, one has nevertheless asked a question about a particular person, a question that it is possible for someone to answer. Contrast this with the use of the same question by the chairman of the local Teetotalers Union. He has just been informed that a man is drinking a martini at their annual party. He responds by asking his informant, "Who is the man drinking a martini?" In asking the question the chairman does not have some particular person in mind about whom he asks the question; if no one is drinking a martini, if the information is wrong, no person can be singled out as the person about whom the question was asked. Unlike the first case, the attribute of being the man drinking a martini is all-important, because if it is the attribute of no one, the chairman's question has no straightforward answer.

This illustrates also another difference between the referential and the attributive use of definite descriptions. In the one case we have asked a question about a particular person or thing even though nothing fits the description we used; in the other this is not so. But also in the one case our question can be answered; in the other it cannot be. In the referential use of a definite description we may succeed in picking out a person or thing to ask a question about even though he or it does not really fit the description; but in the attributive use if nothing fits the description, no straightforward answer to the question can be given.

This further difference is also illustrated by commands or orders containing definite descriptions. Consider the order, "Bring me the book on the table." If "the book on the table" is being used referentially, it is possible to fulfill the order even though there is no book on the table. If, for example, there is a book *beside* the table, though there is none *on* it, one might bring that book back and ask the issuer of the order whether this is "the book you meant." And it may be. But imagine we are told that someone has laid a book on our prize antique table, where nothing should be put. The order, "Bring me the book on the table" cannot now be obeyed unless there is a book that has been placed on the table. There is no possibility of bringing back a book which was never on the table and having it be the one that was meant, because there is no book that in that sense was "meant." In the one case the definite description was a device for getting the other person to pick the right book; if he is able to pick the right book even though it does not satisfy the description, one still succeeds in his purpose. In the other case, there is, antecedently, no "right book" except one which fits the description; the attribute of being the book on the table is essential. Not only is there no book about which an order was issued, if there is no book on the table, but the order itself cannot be obeyed. When a definite description is used attributively in a command or question and nothing fits the description, the command cannot be obeyed and the question cannot be answered. This suggests some analogous consequence for assertions containing definite descriptions used attributively. Perhaps the analogous result is that the assertion is neither true nor false: this is Strawson's view of what happens when the presupposition of the use of a definite description is false. But if so, Strawson's view works not for definite descriptions used referentially, but for the quite different use, which I have called the attributive use.

I have tried to bring out the two uses of definite descriptions by pointing out the different consequences of supposing that nothing fits the description used. There are still other differences. One is this: when a definite description is used referentially, not only is there in some sense a presupposition or implication that someone or something fits the description, as there is also in the attributive use, but there is a quite different presupposition; the speaker presupposes of some *particular* someone or something that he or it fits the description. In asking, for example, "Who is the man drinking a martini?" where we mean to ask a question about that man over there, we are presupposing that that man over there is drinking a martini—not just that *someone* is a man drinking a martini. When we say, in a context where it is clear we are referring to Jones, "Smith's murderer is insane," we are presupposing that Jones is Smith's murderer. No such presupposition is present in the attributive use of definite descriptions. There is, of course, the presupposition that someone *or other* did the murder, but the speaker does not presuppose of someone in particular—Jones or Robinson, say—that he did it. What I mean by this second kind of presupposition that someone or something in particular fits the description—which is present in a referential use but not in an attributive use—can perhaps be seen more clearly by considering a member of the speaker's audience who believes that Smith was not murdered at all. Now in the case of the referential use of the description, "Smith's murderer," he could accuse the speaker of mistakenly presupposing both that someone or other is the murderer and that also Jones is the murderer, for even though he believes Jones not to have done the deed, he knows that the speaker was referring to Jones. But in the case of the attributive use, he can accuse the speaker of having only the first, less specific presupposition; he cannot pick out some person and claim that the speaker is presupposing that that person is Smith's murderer. Now the more particular presuppositions that we find present in referential uses are clearly not ones we can assign to a definite description in some particular sentence in isolation from a context of use. In order to know that a person presupposes that Jones is Smith's murderer in using the sentence "Smith's murderer is insane," we have to know that he is using the description referentially and also to whom he is referring. The sentence by itself does not tell us any of this.

IV

From the way in which I set up each of the previous examples it might be supposed that the important difference between the referential and the attributive use lies in the beliefs of the speaker. Does he believe of some particular person or thing that he or it fits the description used? In the Smith murder example, for instance, there was in the one case no belief as to who did the deed, whereas in the contrasting case it was believed that Jones did it. But this is, in fact, not an essential difference. It is possible for a definite description to be used attributively even though the speaker (and his audience) believes that a certain person or thing fits the description. And it is possible for a definite description to be used referentially where the speaker believes that nothing fits the description. It is true—and this is why, for simplicity, I set up the examples the way I did—that if a speaker does not believe that anything fits the description or does not believe that he is in a position to pick out what does fit the description, it is likely that he is not using it referentially. It is also true that if he and his audience would pick out some particular thing or person as fitting the description, then a use of the definite description is very likely referential. But these are only presumptions and not entailments.

To use the Smith murder case again, suppose that Jones is on trial for the murder and I and everyone else believe him guilty. Suppose that I comment that the murderer of Smith is insane, but instead of backing this up, as in the example previously used, by citing Jones's behavior in the dock, I go on to outline reasons for thinking that *anyone* who murdered poor Smith in that particularly horrible way must be insane. If now it turns out that Jones was not the murderer after all, but someone else was, I think I can claim to have been right if the true murderer is after all insane. Here, I think, I would be using the definite description attributively, even though I believe that a particular person fits the description.

It is also possible to think of cases in which the speaker does not believe that what he means to refer to by using the definite description fits the description, or to imagine cases in which the definite description is used referentially even though the speaker believes *nothing* fits the description. Admittedly, these cases may be parasitic on a more normal use; nevertheless, they are sufficient to show that such beliefs of the speaker are not decisive as to which use is made of a definite description.

Suppose the throne is occupied by a man I firmly believe to be not the king, but a usurper. Imagine also that his followers as firmly believe that he is the king. Suppose I wish to see this man. I might say to his minions, "Is the king in his countinghouse?" I succeed in referring to the man I wish to refer to without myself believing that he fits the description. It is not even necessary, moreover, to suppose that his followers believe him to be the king. If they are cynical about the whole thing, know he is not the king, I may still succeed in referring to the man I wish to refer to. Similarly, neither I nor the people I speak to may suppose that *anyone* is the king and, finally, each party may know that the other does not so suppose and yet the reference may go through.

V

Both the attributive and the referential use of definite descriptions seem to carry a presupposition or implication that there is something which fits the description. But the reasons for the existence of the presupposition or implication are different in the two cases.

There is a presumption that a person who uses a definite description referentially believes that what he wishes to refer to fits the description. Because the purpose of using the description is to get the audience to pick out or think of the right thing or person, one would normally choose a description that he believes the thing or person fits. Normally a misdescription of that to which one wants to refer would mislead the audience. Hence, there is a presumption that the speaker believes *something* fits the description—namely, that to which he refers.

When a definite description is used attributively, however, there is not the same possibility of misdescription. In the example of "Smith's murderer" used attributively, there was not the possibility of misdescribing Jones or anyone else; we were not referring to Jones nor to anyone else by using the description. The presumption that the speaker believes *someone* is Smith's murderer does not arise here from a more specific presumption that he believes Jones or Robinson or someone else whom he can name or identify is Smith's murderer.

The presupposition or implication is borne by a definite description used attributively because if nothing fits the description the linguistic purpose of the speech act will be thwarted. That is, the speaker will not succeed in saying something true, if he makes an assertion; he will not succeed in asking a question that can be answered, if he has asked a question; he will not succeed in issuing an order that can be obeyed, if he has issued an order. If one states that Smith's murderer is insane, when Smith has no murderer, and uses the definite description nonreferentially, then one fails to say anything *true*. If one issues the order "Bring me Smith's murderer" under similar circumstances, the order cannot be obeyed; nothing would count as obeying it.

When the definite description is used referentially, on the other hand, the presupposition or implication stems simply from the fact that normally a person tries to describe correctly what he wants to refer to because normally this is the best way to get his audience to recognize what he is referring to. As we have seen, it is possible for the linguistic purpose of the speech act to be accomplished in such a case even though nothing fits the description; it is possible to say something true or to ask a question that gets answered or to issue a command that gets obeyed. For when the definite description is used referentially, one's audience may succeed in seeing to what one refers even though neither it nor anything else fits the description.

VI

The result of the last section shows something to be wrong with the theories of both Russell and Strawson; for though they give differing accounts of the implication or presupposition involved, each gives only one. Yet, as I have argued, the presupposition or implication is present for a quite different reason, depending upon whether the definite description is used attributively or referentially, and exactly what presuppositions or implications are involved is also different. Moreover, neither theory seems a correct characterization of the referential use. On Russell's there is a logical entailment: "The ϕ is ψ" entails "There exists one and only one ϕ." Whether or not this is so for the attributive use, it does not seem true of the referential use of the definite description. The "implication" that something is the ϕ, as I have argued, does not amount to an entailment; it is more like a presumption based on what is *usually* true of the use of a definite description to refer. In any case, of course, Russell's theory does not show—what is true of the referential use—that the implication that *something* is the ϕ comes from the more specific implication that *what is being referred to* is the ϕ. Hence, as a theory of definite descriptions, Russell's view seems to apply, if at all, to the attributive use only.

Russell's definition of denoting (a definite description denotes an entity if that entity fits the description uniquely) is clearly applicable to either use of definite descriptions. Thus whether or not a definite description is used referentially or attributively, it may have a denotation. Hence, denoting and referring, as I have explicated the latter notion, are distinct and Russell's view recognizes only the former. It seems to me, moreover, that this is a welcome result, that denoting and referring should not be confused. If one tried to maintain that they are the same notion, one result would be that a speaker might be referring to something without knowing it. If someone said, for example, in 1960 before he had any idea that Mr. Goldwater would be the Republican nominee in 1964, "The Republican candidate for president in 1964 will be a conservative" (perhaps on the basis of an analysis of the views of party leaders), the definite description here would *denote* Mr. Goldwater. But would we wish to say that the speaker had referred to, mentioned, or talked about Mr. Goldwater? I feel these terms would be out of place. Yet if we identify referring and denoting, it ought to be possible for it to turn out (after the Republican Convention) that the speaker had, unknown to himself, referred in 1960 to Mr. Goldwater. On my view, however, while the definite description used did *denote* Mr. Goldwater (using Russell's definition), the speaker used it *attributively* and did not *refer* to Mr. Goldwater.

Turning to Strawson's theory, it was supposed to demonstrate how definite descriptions are referential. But it goes too far in this direction. For there are nonreferential uses of definite descriptions also, even as they occur in one and the same sentence. I believe that Strawson's theory involves the following propositions:

(1) If someone asserts that the ϕ is ψ he has not made a true or false statement if there is no ϕ.[10]

(2) If there is no ϕ then the speaker has failed to refer to anything.[11]

(3) The reason he has said nothing true or false is that he has failed to refer.

Each of these propositions is either false or, at best, applies to only one of the two uses of definite descriptions.

Proposition (1) is possibly true of the attributive use. In the example in which "Smith's murderer is insane" was said when Smith's body was first discovered, an attributive use of the definite description, there was no person to whom the speaker referred. If Smith had no murderer, nothing true was said. It is quite tempting to conclude, following Strawson, that nothing true *or* false was said. But where the definite description is used referentially, something true may well have been said. It is possible that something true was said of the person or thing referred to.[12]

Proposition (2) is, as we have seen, simply false. Where a definite description is used referentially it is perfectly possible to refer to something though nothing fits the description used.

The situation with proposition (3) is a bit more complicated. It ties together, on Strawson's view, the two strands given in (1) and (2). As an account of why, when the presupposition is false, nothing true or false has been stated, it clearly cannot work for the attributive use of definite descriptions, for the reason it supplies is that reference has failed. It does not then give the reason why, if indeed this is so, a speaker using a definite description attributively fails to say anything true or false if nothing fits the description. It does, however, raise a question about the referential use. Can reference fail when a definite description is used referentially?

I do not fail to refer merely because my audience does not correctly pick out what I am referring to. I can be referring to a particular man when I use the description "the man drinking a martini," even though the people to whom I speak fail to pick out the right person or any person at all. Nor, as we have stressed, do I fail to refer when nothing fits the description. But perhaps I fail to refer in some extreme circumstances, when there is nothing that *I* am willing to pick out as that to which I referred.

Suppose that I think I see at some distance a man walking and ask, "Is the man carrying a walking stick the professor of history?" We should perhaps distinguish four cases at this point: (a) There is a man carrying a walking stick; I have then referred to a person and asked a question about him that can be answered if my audience has the information. (b) The man over there is not carrying a walking stick, but an umbrella; I have still referred to someone and asked a question that can be answered, though if my audience sees that it is an umbrella and not a walking stick, they may also correct my apparently mistaken impression. (c) It is not a man at all, but a rock that looks like one; in this case, I think I still have referred to something, to the thing over there that happens to be a rock but that I took to be a man. But in this case it is not clear that my question can be answered correctly. This, I think, is not because I have failed to refer, but rather because, given the true nature of what I referred to, my question is not appropriate. A simple "No, that is not the professor of history" is at least a bit misleading if said by someone who realizes that I mistook a rock for a person. It may, therefore, be plausible to conclude that in such a case I have not asked a question to which there is a straightforwardly correct answer. But if this is true, it is not because nothing fits the description I used, but rather because what I referred to is a rock and my question has no correct answer when asked of a rock. (d) There is finally the case in which there is nothing at all where I thought there was a man with a walking stick; and perhaps here we have a genuine failure to refer at all, even though the description was used for the purpose of referring. There is no rock, nor anything else, to which I meant to refer; it was, perhaps, a trick of light that made me think there was a man there. I cannot say of anything, "That is what I was referring to, though I now see that it's not a man carrying a walking stick." This failure of reference, however, requires circumstances much more radical than the mere nonexistence of anything fitting the description used. It requires that there be nothing of which it can be said, "That is what he was referring to." Now perhaps also in such cases, if the speaker has asserted something, he fails to state anything true or false if there is nothing that can be identified as that to which he referred. But if so, the failure of reference and truth value does not come about merely because nothing fits the description he used. So (3) may be true of some cases of the referential use of definite descriptions; it may be true that a failure of reference results in a lack of truth value. But these cases are of a much more extreme sort than Strawson's theory implies.

I conclude, then, that neither Russell's nor Strawson's theory represents a correct account of the use of definite descriptions—Russell's because it ignores altogether the referential use, Strawson's because it fails to make the distinction between the referential and the attributive and mixes together truths about each (together with some things that are false).

VII

It does not seem possible to say categorically of a definite description in a particular sentence that it is a referring expression (of course, one could say this if he meant that it *might* be used to refer). In general, whether or not a definite description is used referentially or attributively is a function of the speaker's intentions in a particular case. "The murderer of Smith" may be used either way in the sentence "The murderer of Smith is insane." It does not appear plausible to account for this, either, as an ambiguity in the sentence. The grammatical structure of the sentence seems to me to be the same whether the description is used referentially or attributively: that is, it is not syntactically ambiguous. Nor does it seem at all attractive to suppose an ambiguity in the meaning of the words; it does not appear to be semantically ambiguous. (Perhaps we could say that the sentence is pragmatically ambiguous: the distinction between roles that the description plays is a function of the speaker's intentions.) These, of course, are intuitions; I do not have an argument for these conclusions. Nevertheless, the burden of proof is surely on the other side.

This, I think, means that the view, for example, that sentences can be divided up into predicates, logical operators, and referring expressions is not generally true. In the case of definite descriptions one cannot always assign the referential function in isolation from a particular occasion on which it is used.

There may be sentences in which a definite description can be used only attributively or only referentially. A sentence in which it seems that the definite description could be used only attributively would be "Point out the man who is drinking my martini." I am not so certain that any can be found in which the definite description can be used only referentially. Even if there are such sentences, it does not spoil the point that there are many sentences, apparently not ambiguous either syntactically or semantically, containing definite descriptions that can be used either way.

If it could be shown that the dual use of definite descriptions can be accounted for by the presence of an ambiguity, there is still a point to be made against the theories of Strawson and Russell. For neither, so far as I can see, has anything to say about the possibility of such an ambiguity and, in fact, neither seems compatible with such a possibility. Russell's does not recognize the possibility of the referring use, and Strawson's, as I have tried to show in the last section, combines elements from each use into one unitary account.

Thus the view that there is an ambiguity in such sentences does not seem any more attractive to these positions.

VIII

Using a definite description referentially, a speaker may say something true even though the description correctly applies to nothing. The sense in which he may say something true is the sense in which he may say something true about someone or something. This sense is, I think, an interesting one that needs investigation. Isolating it is one of the by-products of the distinction between the attributive and referential uses of definite descriptions.

For one thing, it raises questions about the notion of a statement. This is brought out by considering a passage in a paper by Leonard Linsky in which he rightly makes the point that one can refer to someone although the definite description used does not correctly describe the person:

> ... said of a spinster that "Her husband is kind to her" is neither true nor false. But a speaker might very well be referring to someone using these words, for he may think that someone is the husband of the lady (who in fact is a spinster). Still, the statement is neither true nor false, for it presupposes that the lady has a husband, which she has not. This last refutes Strawson's thesis that if the presupposition of existence is not satisfied, the speaker has failed to refer.[13]

There is much that is right in this passage. But because Linsky does not make the distinction between the referential and the attributive uses of definite descriptions, it does not represent a wholly adequate account of the situation. A perhaps minor point about this passage is that Linsky apparently thinks it sufficient to establish that the speaker in his example is referring to someone by using the definite description "her husband," that he *believe* that someone is her husband. This will only approximate the truth provided that the "someone" in the description of the belief means "someone in particular" and is not merely the existential quantifier, "there is someone or other." For in both the attributive and the referential use the belief that someone *or other* is the husband of the lady is very likely to be present. If, for example, the speaker has just met the lady and, noticing her cheerfulness and radiant good health, makes his remark from his conviction that these attributes are always the result of having good husbands, he would be using the definite description attributively. Since she has no husband, there is no one to pick out as the person to whom he was referring. Nevertheless, the speaker believed that *someone or other* was her husband. On the other hand, if the use of "her husband" was simply a way of referring to a man the speaker has just met whom he assumed to be the lady's husband, he would have referred to that man even though neither he nor anyone else fits the description. I think it is likely that in this passage Linsky did mean by "someone," in his description of the belief, "someone in particular." But even then, as we have seen, we have neither a sufficient nor a necessary condition for a referential use of the definite description. A definite description can be used attributively even when the speaker believes that some particular thing or person fits the description, and it can be used referentially in the absence of this belief.

My main point, here, however, has to do with Linsky's view that because the presupposition is not satisfied, the *statement* is neither true nor false. This seems to me possibly correct *if* the definite description is thought of as being used attributively (depending upon whether we go with Strawson or Russell). But when we consider it as used referentially, this categorical assertion is no longer clearly correct. For the man the speaker referred to may indeed be kind to the spinster; the speaker may have said something true about that man. Now the difficulty is in the notion of "the statement." Suppose that we know that the lady is a spinster, but nevertheless know that the man referred to by the speaker is kind to her. It seems to me that we shall, on the one hand, want to hold that the speaker said something true, but be reluctant to express this by "It is true that her husband is kind to her."

This shows, I think, a difficulty in speaking simply about "the statement" when definite descriptions are used referentially. For the speaker stated something, in this example, about a particular person, and his statement, we may suppose, was true. Nevertheless, we should not like to agree with his statement by using the sentence he used; we should not like to identify the true statement via the speaker's words. The reason for this is not so hard to find. If we say, in this example, "It is true that her husband is kind to her," *we* are now using the definite description either attributively or referentially. But we should not be subscribing to what the original speaker truly said if we use the description attributively, for it was only in its function as referring to a particular person that the definite description yields the possibility of saying something true (since the lady has no husband). Our reluctance, however, to endorse the original speaker's statement by using the definite description referentially to refer to the same person stems from quite a different consideration. For if we too were laboring under the mistaken belief that this man was the lady's husband, we could agree with the original speaker using his exact words. (Moreover, it is possible, as we have seen, deliberately to use a definite description to refer to someone we believe not to fit the description.) Hence, our reluctance to use the original speaker's words does not arise from the fact that if we did we should not succeed in stating anything true or false. It rather stems from the fact that when a definite description is used referentially there is a presumption that the speaker believes that what he refers to fits the description. Since we, who know the lady to be a spinster, would not normally want to give the impression that we believe otherwise, we would not like to use the original speaker's way of referring to the man in question.

How then would we express agreement with the original speaker without involving ourselves in unwanted impressions about our beliefs? The answer shows another difference between the referential and attributive uses of definite descriptions and brings out an important point about genuine referring.

When a speaker says, "The ϕ is ψ," where "the ϕ" is used attributively, if there is no ϕ, we cannot correctly report the speaker as having said *of* this or that person or thing that it is ψ. But if the definite description is used referentially we can report the speaker as having attributed ψ to something. And *we* may refer to what the speaker referred to, using whatever description or name suits our purpose. Thus, if a speaker says, "Her husband is kind to her," referring to the man he was just talking to, and if that man is Jones, we may report him as having said *of Jones* that he is kind to her. If Jones is also the president of the college, we may report the speaker as having said *of the president of the college* that he is kind to her. And finally, if we are talking to Jones, we may say, referring to the original speaker, "He said of you that *you* are kind to her." It does not matter here whether or not the woman has a husband or whether, if she does, Jones is her husband. If the original speaker referred to Jones, he said of him that he is kind to her. Thus where the definite description is used referentially, but does not fit what was referred to, we can report what a speaker said and agree with him by using a description or name which does fit. In doing so we need not, it is important to note, choose a description or name which the original speaker would agree fits what he was referring to. That is, we can report the speaker in the above case to have said truly of Jones that he is kind to her even if the original speaker did not know that the man he was referring to is named Jones or even if he thinks he is not named Jones.

Returning to what Linsky said in the passage quoted, he claimed that, were someone to say "Her husband is kind to her," when she has no husband, *the statement* would be neither true nor false. As I have said, this is a likely view to hold if the definite description is being used attributively. But if it is being used referentially it is not clear what is meant by "the statement." If we think about what the speaker said about the person he referred to, then there is no reason to suppose he has not said something true or false about him, even though he is not the lady's husband. And Linsky's claim would be wrong. On the other hand, if we do not identify the statement in this way, what is the statement that the speaker made? To say that the statement he made was that her husband is kind to her lands us in difficulties. For we have to decide whether in using the definite description here in the identification of the statement, we are using it attributively or referentially. If the former, then we misrepresent the linguistic performance of the speaker; if the latter, then we are ourselves referring to someone and reporting the speaker to have said something of that person, in which case we are back to the possibility that he did say something true or false of that person.

I am thus drawn to the conclusion that when a speaker uses a definite description referentially he may have stated something true or false even if nothing fits the description, and that there is not a clear sense in which he has made a statement which is neither true nor false.

IX

I want to end by a brief examination of a picture of what a genuine referring expression is that one might derive from Russell's views. I want to suggest that this picture is not so far wrong as one might suppose and that strange as this may seem, some of the things we have said about the referential use of definite descriptions are not foreign to this picture.

Genuine proper names, in Russell's sense, would refer to something without ascribing any properties to it. They would, one might say, refer to the thing itself, not simply the thing insofar as it falls under a certain description.[14] Now this would seem to Russell something a definite description could not do, for he assumed that if definite descriptions were capable of referring at all, they would refer to something only insofar as that thing satisfied the description. Not only have we seen this assumption to be false, however, but in the last section we saw something more. We saw that when a definite description is used referentially, a speaker can be reported as having said something *of* something. And in reporting what it was of which he said something we are not restricted to the description he used, or synonyms of it; we may ourselves refer to it using any descriptions, names, and so forth, that will do the job. Now this seems to give a sense in which we are concerned with the thing itself and not just the thing under a certain description, when we report the linguistic act of a speaker using a definite description referentially. That is, such a definite description comes closer to performing the function of Russell's proper names than certainly he supposed.

Russell thought, I believe, that whenever we use descriptions, as opposed to proper names, we introduce an element of generality which ought to be absent if what we are doing is referring to some particular thing. This is clear from his analysis of sentences containing definite descriptions. One of the conclusions we are supposed to draw from that analysis is that such sentences express what are in reality completely general propositions: there is a ϕ and only one such and any ϕ is ψ. We might put this in a slightly different way. If there is anything which might be identified as reference here, it is reference in a very weak sense—namely, reference to *whatever* is the one and only one ϕ, if there is any such. Now this is something we might well say about the attributive use of definite descriptions, as should be evident from the previous discussion. But this lack of particularity is absent from the referential use of definite descriptions precisely because the description is here merely a device for getting one's audience to pick out or think of the thing to be spoken about, a device which may serve its function even if the description is incorrect. More importantly perhaps, in the referential use as opposed to the attributive, there is a *right* thing to be picked out by the audience and its being the right thing is not simply a function of its fitting the description.

NOTES

1. I should like to thank my colleagues, John Canfield, Sydney Shoemaker, and Timothy Smiley, who read an earlier draft and gave me helpful suggestions. I also had the benefit of the valuable and detailed comments of the referee for the paper, to whom I wish to express my gratitude.
2. "On Denoting," reprinted in *Logic and Knowledge*, ed. by Robert C. Marsh (London, 1956), p. 51.
3. "On Referring," reprinted in *Philosophy and Ordinary Language*, ed. by Charles C. Caton (Urbana, 1963), pp. 162–63.
4. Ibid., p. 162.
5. Ibid., p. 170.
6. Here and elsewhere I use the disjunction "presuppose or imply" to avoid taking a stand that would side me with Russell or Strawson on the issue of what the relationship involved is. To take a stand here would be beside my main point as

well as being misleading, since later on I shall argue that the presupposition orimplication arises in a different way depending upon the use to which the definite description is put. This last also accounts for my use of the vagueness indicator, "in some sense."

7. In a footnote added to the original version of "On Referring" (*op. cit.*, p. 181) Strawson seems to imply that where the presupposition is false, we still succeed in referring in a "secondary" way, which seems to mean "as we could be said to refer to fictional or make-believe things." But his view is still that we cannot refer in such a case in the "primary" way. This is, I believe, wrong. For a discussion of this modification of Strawson's view see Charles C. Caton, "Strawson on Referring," *Mind*, LXVIII (1959), 539–44.
8. This is an adaptation of an example (used for a somewhat different purpose) given by Leonard Linsky in "Reference and Referents," in *Philosophy and Ordinary Language*, p. 80.
9. In "Reference and Referents" (pp. 74–75, 80), Linsky correctly points out that one does not fail to refer simply because the description used does not in fact fit anything (or fits more than one thing). Thus he pinpoints one of the difficulties in Strawson's view. Here, however, I use this fact about referring to make a distinction I believe he does not draw, between two uses of definite descriptions. I later discuss the second passage from Linsky's paper.
10. In "A Reply to Mr. Sellars," *Philosophical Review*, LXIII (1954), 216–31, Strawson admits that we do not always refuse to ascribe truth to what a person says when the definite description he uses fails to fit anything (or fits more than one thing). To cite one of his examples, a person who said, "The United States Chamber of Deputies contains representatives of two major parties," would be allowed to have said something true even though he had used the wrong title. Strawson thinks this does not constitute a genuine problem for his view. He thinks that what we do in such cases, "where the speaker's intended reference is pretty clear, is simply to amend his statement in accordance with his guessed intentions and assess the amended statement for truth or falsity; we are not awarding a truth value at all to the original statement" (p. 230).

    The notion of an "amended statement," however, will not do. We may note, first of all, that the sort of case Strawson has in mind could arise only when a definite description is used referentially. For the "amendment" is made by seeing the speaker's intended reference. But this could happen only if the speaker had an intended reference, a particular person or thing in mind, independent of the description he used. The cases Strawson has in mind are presumably not cases of slips of the tongue or the like; presumably they are cases in which a definite description is used because the speaker believes, though he is mistaken, that he is describing correctly what he wants to refer to. We supposedly amend the statement by knowing to what he intends to refer. But what description is to be used in the amended statement? In the example, perhaps, we could use "the United States Congress." But this description might be one the speaker would not even accept as correctly describing what he wants to refer to, because he is misinformed about the correct title. Hence, this is not a case of deciding what the speaker meant to say as opposed to what he in fact said, for the speaker did not mean to say "the United States Congress." If this is so, then there is no bar to the "amended" statement containing any description that does correctly pick out what the speaker intended to refer to. It could be, e.g., "The lower house of the United States Congress." But this means that there is no one unique "amended" statement to be assessed for truth value. And, in fact, it should now be clear that the notion of the amended statement really plays no role anyway. For if we can arrive at the amended statement only by first knowing to what the speaker intended to refer, we can assess the truth of what he said simply by deciding whether what he intended to refer to has the properties he ascribed to it.

11. As noted earlier (n. 7), Strawson may allow that one has possibly referred in a "secondary" way, but, if I am right, the fact that there is no ϕ does not preclude one from having referred in the same way one does if there is a ϕ.
12. For a further discussion of the notion of saying something true *of* someone or something, see sec. VIII.
13. "Reference and Referents," p. 80. It should be clear that I agree with Linsky in holding that a speaker may refer even though the "presupposition of existence" is not satisfied. And I agree in thinking this an objection to Strawson's view. I think, however, that this point, among others, can be used to define two distinct uses of definite descriptions which, in turn, yields a more general criticism of Strawson. So, while I develop here a point of difference, which grows out of the distinction I want to make, I find myself in agreement with much of Linsky's article.
14. Cf. "The Philosophy of Logical Atomism," reprinted in *Logic and Knowledge*, p. 200.

[2]

PUTTING HUMPTY DUMPTY TOGETHER AGAIN

Who is master, Humpty Dumpty or Humpty Dumpty's language?[1] Mr. MacKay[2] compares some things I said about definite descriptions and reference[3] to Humpty Dumpty's theory of meaning. In doing so, I think the principle he draws from Humpty Dumpty's conversation with Alice is that the conventions of one's language dictate the meaning of one's words, and intentions are powerless to intervene. Since "glory" does not mean "a nice knockdown argument" in the language Humpty Dumpty speaks, he could not have meant that by "glory" nor could "glory" have meant that in the conversation, no matter what intentions he may have had. This has some importance beyond any application to my article, since theories of meaning that take the intentions of speakers as primitive (for example, Grice's view in his article "Meaning")[4] must either deny the principle or show how they avoid running afoul of it. MacKay, of course, uses Humpty Dumpty only for the purpose of drawing an analogy and there is no reason to suppose that what I said about reference commits me to any theory of meaning. Nevertheless, I will

First published in *The Philosophical Review*, 1968, 77: 213–15.

have something to say about the significance of Humpty Dumpty's conversation with Alice and about Wittgenstein's challenge to "*Say* 'It's cold here' and mean 'It's hot here,'" because it is easy to make a mistake about them very similar to one I find in MacKay's criticisms of my treatment of reference.

First, however, I want to discuss the connection between what MacKay says about reference and my article. The purpose of the article he discusses was to make a distinction between two uses of definite descriptions. MacKay does not deal with the distinction itself; instead, he criticizes some things I said about reference in the course of drawing it. Nevertheless, what he says may seem to cast doubt on the existence of a difference between two uses of definite descriptions, though I am not sure whether that was his purpose. In any case, it turns out that MacKay's view can be shown to presuppose the distinction. To show this will require a brief look at how I attempted to draw it.

In the article in question, I pointed out several features of what I called the "referential" use of definite descriptions not shared with another use of them, which I called the "attributive" use. The two uses can be thought of as corresponding to two possible purposes a speaker may have in using a definite description. Looking at the referential use first, a speaker may wish to attribute a property to, ask a question about, issue an order concerning some particular person, object, situation, and so forth. We can view his task as that of finding a description suitable for allowing his audience to identify that person, object, situation, and so forth. The description chosen need not be unique; a speaker will often use some description such as "the table," leaving it to his audience to determine from context or from a knowledge of the speaker's likely wants, beliefs, and so forth to which table he is referring.[5] The description chosen may be different for different audiences. Suppose, for example, that a speaker wants to relate an amusing thing done by Jones. To one audience he might begin, "The man I introduced to you yesterday . . . ," to another "Our mutual friend . . . ," to still another "The man you see over there. . . ." The distinguishing characteristic of the referential use is the existence of an entity the speaker wants to talk about and in relation to which he chooses a description as a means of referring to it. There is a sense in which the particular description chosen is inessential, though not irrelevant, to what the speaker accomplishes, in this case, telling something about Jones. The following is a familiar sort of conversation in which a speaker shows his willingness to abandon one description for another when it becomes evident that the first is not fulfilling its purpose of identifying for the audience the reference of the speaker's remarks: "The man I introduced to you yesterday did an amusing thing." "I don't recall your introducing anyone to me." "Well, perhaps I didn't, but don't you remember the man in the loud checked suit?" "Oh, now I know whom you mean."

In contrast, a definite description used attributively is not in the same way dispensable; it is essential to the purpose of the speech act. As an illustration, suppose someone to make a wager, expressing his side of the bet in the words, "The winner of the Indianapolis 500 race drove a turbine-powered car." The speaker could intend his bet to be understood not as being a bet about, say, Parnelli Jones or any other race driver, but about the winner whoever he may have been. And this could be so even if he happens to have a belief about who won the race (though, of course, he need have none). Suppose that he believes Parnelli Jones won the race; nevertheless he will expect to collect even if this belief is mistaken so long as whoever won the race did drive a turbine-powered car, and he will lose if whoever won drove an ordinary car even though Jones's car was turbine-powered. It would be inappropriate and irrelevant to the bet for the speaker to try out a new description—for example, "the man in the red car," when his belief about who won the race turns out to be mistaken. Similarly, if there were no winner of the 500—the race having been called before the finish—the speaker could not appropriately turn to another description, as the speaker did in the previous example when it turned out that he had not introduced anyone. Finally, if Parnelli Jones was the winner, one can still say that *had* he not been the winner, then what kind of car *he* drove would have been irrelevant to the bet.

The central difference between the two uses of definite descriptions that emerges is this. In connection with an attributive use, if we want to identify some entity as what the speaker was talking about in using the definite description, the only candidate would be something that satisfies the description. A referential use, however, allows of another possibility—that the entity the speaker was talking about does not in fact satisfy the description. When the entity so identified does fit the description, it can nevertheless be said that had it not done so, it still would have been what the speaker was talking about. Sometimes we want to say something about an entity and try to identify it for our audience via a description of it, thus making it a possibility that the entity and description do not match up. At other times we want to talk about whatever fits a certain description (uniquely) and then there is no possibility of an entity that is at once what we wanted to talk about but not correctly characterized by the description.

As a consequence of this difference several things seemed to me to be true of a referential use that are not true of an attributive use. These were discussed in some detail in the article MacKay criticizes, so they will only be listed here. If a speaker *S* uses a definite description, "the φ," referentially there will be some entity *e* (or, at least, the speaker will intend that there should be) about which the following will be true. (I assume that an assertion was made. Appropriate changes would be required for questions, commands, and so forth.)

(1) *S* will have referred to *e* whether or not *e* is in fact φ.
(2) *S* will have said something true or false about *e* whether or not *e* is in fact φ (provided that everything is in order concerning the remainder of the speech act).
(3) *S*, in using "the φ" to refer to *e*, will have presupposed or implied that *e* is φ.
(4) In reporting *S*'s speech act, it will be correct to say that he stated something about *e* and in reporting this to use expressions to refer to *e* other than "the φ" or synonyms of it.[6]

Had the definite description been used attributively there would be no such entity *e* (nor would the speaker have intended that there should be).

The first of these characteristics is the one that bothers MacKay. His view, I believe, can be summed up in the following four points:

(*A*) Referring is one way among others of making it known what a speaker is talking about.
(*B*) In using a definite description to refer, one succeeds in referring only to something that fits the description used (barring, perhaps, "near misses").
(*C*) What one is talking about, however, may fail altogether to fit the description used.
(*D*) In that case, in view of (*B*), one does not succeed in *referring* to what one is talking about, although one may succeed in making it *knowable* what one is talking about.

Looking at points (*C*) and (*D*) one will notice that MacKay is describing a use of definite descriptions for which it is possible to distinguish an entity the speaker is talking about independently of the description he uses—an entity, that is, that may not fit the description. Now the use of definite descriptions that I call "referential" provides for just such a possibility. If then it can be shown that there are uses of definite descriptions, in fact those that I call "attributive," for which no such possibility exists, MacKay's view must itself yield the very distinction I wanted to make. It will still be true, of course, that there is an issue. If he is correct, the referential use of definite descriptions lacks at least one of the features I thought it had. But the distinction itself would not only remain in the face of his criticism, it would, in fact, be presupposed by it.

In his discussion, then, MacKay uses the possibility that what a speaker is talking about may fail to fit the description he uses. But looking at the example of the attributive use given above, we find that this possibility is not present. A wager is made, expressed in the words, "The winner of the Indianapolis 500 drove a turbine-powered car." The bettor collects, we imagine, if and only if the race was won by a driver in a turbine-powered car, regardless of which driver that may have been. Throughout his paper, MacKay uses the notion of "what the speaker was talking about." This is an extremely flexible expression, with many uses.[7] In our example, it seems natural to say that the speaker was talking about the winner of the Indianapolis 500 race (and that the bet was a bet about the winner of this race). But the expression "*X* was talking about *Y*," as it finds application in this example, is an intentional or "referentially opaque" context with respect to "*Y*." Suppose that Smith was a driver in the race. In making the wager in question, could the speaker have been talking about Smith? If Smith was not the winner of the race, then certainly there seems to be no sense in which the speaker was talking about him (and the bet was not a bet about Smith). Even if, at the time of the bet, the speaker believed Smith to be the winning driver, he was not, I think, talking about him.[8] This is enough to show that in this use of a definite description there is not the possibility that the speaker is talking about an entity that, in fact, fails to fit the description he uses. It seems to me, moreover, that even if Smith was the winner of the race, the speaker was not talking about him. From "The speaker was talking about the winner of the race" and "Smith was the winner of the race," it does not follow, in this case, that the speaker was talking about Smith.

To state his view about reference and definite descriptions, MacKay employed a notion of "what the speaker is talking about" that is extensional and allows for the possibility that what the speaker is talking about is an entity that fails to fit the description he used. But this notion is applicable only to some uses of definite descriptions and these would have to be distinguished from those to which it does not apply. Working out this distinction, however, would simply give us another way of getting at the difference between the "referential" and the "attributive" use of definite descriptions.

MacKay notes that in my paper many of the examples of a speaker referring to something that does not fit the description used are what he calls "near misses." Could I have sustained my point, he wonders, had I instead considered examples in which what the speaker intended to refer to was very far from fitting the description?[9] Before dealing with this directly, however, I want to comment on another question raised by the subject of near misses.

In my paper I suggested that when a speaker uses a definite description, "the φ," referentially to refer to something, e, he may have said something true about e even if e is not φ or even if nothing is φ. In contrast, I thought, if the definite description is used attributively, then if nothing is φ, the speaker cannot have said something true (I left it open whether he would then have said something false). The reason for this difference is that in the case of the attributive use there is no entity e standing as the referent whether or not it fits the description, and so there is nothing for the speaker to have predicated something of when nothing satisfies the description. But this does not take account of near misses and so is, perhaps, too rigid in relation to our actual practice in such cases. In one example of the attributive use in my paper, a person upon finding the body of his friend Smith exclaims, "Smith's murderer is insane." In the example, the speaker had no particular person in mind as Smith's murderer. I then asked what the consequences were if Smith in fact had not been murdered and I suggested that the speaker could not have said something true. But suppose that while Smith did die of natural causes, he had indeed been assaulted before death and that the evidence that led the speaker to attribute insanity to "Smith's murderer" is still good evidence that his assailant is insane. In a sense the speaker has scored a "near miss." Are we prepared to say flatly that the speaker did not state the truth? Since some of my examples of referential uses of definite descriptions also involved in some sense "near misses," this sort of consideration has led several people to wonder whether there is any difference between the two uses along these lines.

But if I ignored the possibility of near misses in connection with what I called "attributive" uses, the distinction is not really harmed. For there are two sources of near misses, one for the attributive use and another for the referential. A near miss occurs with an attributive use when nothing exactly fits the description used, but some individual or other does fit a description in some sense close in meaning to the one used. It is a quite different sort of near miss, however, that is recognized by seeing that the particular individual the speaker wanted to refer to has been described in a slightly inaccurate way. In the one case a near miss is scored, we might say, when the speaker just misses some target or other; in the other when he just misses the target he aimed at. Only in the referential use can a speaker have "missed by a mile," because only that use involves a particular entity that the description either fits neatly, just misses, or misses wildly. Once this is seen, taking near misses into account does not blur the distinction. If anything, it helps one to see what the distinction is.

MacKay holds that when a speaker grossly misdescribes what he wants to talk about, he does not succeed in referring to it. He admits, in a footnote, that this may seem to be no more than a verbal dispute—what he calls "what the speaker is talking about" I call "what the speaker is referring to." If, as I have argued above, his view of the matter yields the distinction in uses of definite descriptions I wanted to draw, why is it not a verbal issue? It is not a question of the ordinary use of the verb "to refer." (I think, in fact, considerations of that sort may be more on my side than his.) Neither of us seems to be analyzing the ordinary use of the term. What then are the unacceptable consequences of adopting my way of talking about such cases?

MacKay imagines someone intending to refer to a book saying, "Bring me the rock on the table." On my view this should be a perfectly clear case of referring to a book. But, he argues, "If one can refer to a book by using 'the rock,' then one can refer to a book by using any *o.r.e.* [ostensible referring expression], and so the actual *o.r.e.* used becomes irrelevant." MacKay's conclusion does not immediately follow. It does not follow from the fact that we can imagine *some* circumstances in which a speaker refers to a book by using the definite description, "the rock," that we can imagine this happening in *any* circumstances. But the latter would be required to make the particular definite description used irrelevant. From what I said in my article it is only in some circumstances that we can imagine a speaker referring to a book by using the definite description, "the rock"—namely, when he really does intend to refer to something which is in fact a book, by using the definite description, "the rock." This may seem hardly any limitation at all, but that,

I believe, is the interesting mistake in MacKay's criticism. I believe the route MacKay's reasoning takes is the following. In the speech acts we are considering, it is the speaker's intention to refer to something. If he can accomplish this when he uses a definite description for that purpose regardless of the content of the description, then the content cannot matter to him—"the actual *o.r.e.* used becomes irrelevant." He might as well use one description as another so long as he uses them with the right intention. And this result is absurd. This is where the analogy with Humpty Dumpty enters. Humpty Dumpty thinks that he invests a word with meaning simply by using it with the intention that it shall mean that. But then it seems that it should be irrelevant to him *what* word he uses. I think this line of reasoning contains a mistake. No such consequence really follows from my way of talking about referring or even from Humpty Dumpty's theory of meaning, whatever other defects there may be in that. Because it has some independent interest, I will begin with Humpty Dumpty's theory.

"Glory" does not mean "a nice knockdown argument" in the language Humpty Dumpty speaks. Does it follow that "glory" could not have meant that in the conversation with Alice? Or that Humpty Dumpty did not mean that by "glory"? It is not my purpose here to defend a theory of *meaning* based on the intentions of speakers. My limited purpose is to suggest that no disastrous consequences follow from the position that what a speaker refers to in a referential use of a definite description is determined by his intentions. (I hope it is obvious that adopting this viewpoint on *reference* does not commit one to any such theory of *meaning*.) Nevertheless, the mistake I believe Mr. MacKay commits in his criticism of what I had to say about reference seems one that it would be easy to commit in thinking about Humpty Dumpty's conversation. If so, it may be of interest to look at it in that connection. In outline, what I want to show is that there is an explanation of the absurdity we find in the exchange with Alice that is compatible with theories of meaning based on the intentions of speakers. Similarly, the inability to respond to Wittgenstein's challenge to "*Say* 'It's cold here' and mean 'It's hot here'" can be explained without subscribing to a particular view such as that meaning can arise only in the context of an established practice. Finally, I will try to show that the availability of this sort of explanation means that speaking of reference in the way I did does not have the consequences MacKay believes it does.

Humpty Dumpty believes himself to be master of the meaning of his words in that if he intends a word to mean such and such then it will mean that when he uses it. MacKay, in making use of what he considers an absurd theory of meaning for the purpose of comparing it to what I said about reference, seems to find no difficulty in the possibility of Humpty Dumpty forming the intention to mean by a word what it does not standardly mean, while at the same time having no reason at all to suppose that his audience, Alice, will understand him. Forming the intention to mean "a nice knockdown argument" by the word "glory" in such circumstances may seem as easy as falling off a wall. Similarly, MacKay finds nothing odd about the possibility that a person should simply intend to refer to a book by the words "the rock." What goes wrong, he seems to think, is that the intention cannot be fulfilled. After all, one might say, what could be easier than forming an intention? And if intentions were sufficient, then a speaker could mean anything by any word at any time or refer to anything using any definite description at any time. Or so it may seem.

The fact about intentions that I want to stress is that they are essentially connected with expectations.[10] Ask someone to flap his arms with the intention of flying. In response he can certainly wave his arms up and down, just as one can easily on command say the words

"It's cold here." But this is not to do it with the intention of flying. Nor does it seem to me that a normal adult in normal circumstances can flap his arms and in doing so really have that intention. Perhaps one can, by a stretch of the imagination, conceive of someone (a child, say, who has seen birds flying) doing this. But such a person—the child, for example—would have expectations not shared with us. Similarly, one cannot say entirely out of the blue, "It's cold here" and mean "It's hot here," but not, I think, because whatever one's intentions the words will not get invested with that meaning. Rather, we can explain this by the impossibility of having the right intention in such circumstances. To the next person who comes in the room I say, "It's cold here." I have no expectations, any more than Humpty Dumpty did about Alice, that the person will construe my words in a novel way. Could I really intend that "cold" should mean "hot"? Or would my performance not be so much arm-flapping?

In the analysis of meaning given by Grice,[11] a speaker means something by an utterance when he has a certain complex kind of intention involving recognition on the part of his audience of his intention. And what the speaker means is determined by the content of that intention. Whether he can form that intention, however, may depend upon what expectations he has about his audience and their ability to grasp his intention. It does not follow, then, from this analysis that speakers might, out of the blue, mean anything at all by any utterance. And the existence of an established practice may be *usually* required for speakers to have the right expectations.

Had Humpty Dumpty prefaced his comment to Alice with an explicit stipulation of what he would mean by the word "glory," the episode could not have been used by Lewis Carroll to raise a problem about meaning. By stating that he would mean "a nice knock-down argument" by "glory," Humpty Dumpty could expect Alice to understand him correctly when he said, "There's glory for you."

I think the episode would also lose its interest if there were in the situation something implicit to make it possible for Humpty Dumpty to expect Alice to grasp his intention. If I were to end this reply to MacKay with the sentence "There's glory for you" I would be guilty of arrogance and, no doubt, of overestimating the strength of what I have said, but given the background I do not think I could be accused of saying something unintelligible. I would be understood, and would I not have meant by "glory" "a nice knockdown argument"? Would not "glory" in that last sentence mean that? It is at least not obvious that it would not. But, for all I know, no one (except possibly Humpty Dumpty) has ever meant that by "glory," and there is not an established practice or convention backing it up. What is strange about Humpty Dumpty's conversation may not be so much the theory of meaning that he seems to have, but rather his wanting us to believe that, without any assumption that Alice might understand him, he really did have that intention about the word "glory." I cannot credit him with that intention any more than I could credit a seemingly rational adult with the intention to fly when I see him flapping his arms up and down.

Returning now to reference, given the way I talked about the referential use of definite descriptions, one can imagine circumstances in which someone refers to a book by using the words "the rock." But it does not follow that, for example, I can now refer to a book by saying to the next person to come into the room, "Please bring me the rock." To think that it does involves the view just now discussed, that there is no difficulty in forming any intention whatever. The reason I cannot say that to the next person I see and refer to a book is the same as the reason I cannot now say to that person, "It's cold here" and mean "It's hot here." I do not have the right expectations about my audience. In the same way I cannot now flap my arms intending to fly. What we have to imagine are situations in which a person does really intend to refer to a book in saying "the rock," and these are not so easy to come by. Most of the examples in my paper of speakers referring to things that do not fit the description used had the speaker believing that what he wanted to refer to did fit the description. Thus, if by a trick of light what is a book looks to me like a rock, I am inclined to say that I would have referred to a book in saying "Bring me the rock." I would, of course, have reason to expect this description to enable my audience to pick out what I was referring to (even though in this case I may be wrong about it). As an extreme case I also thought that one could refer to something knowing that it did not fit the description used, but again when one had certain expectations about the audience. To change the example slightly, suppose there is a rock on my shelf that has been carefully carved to resemble a book and that I know the person I am speaking to cannot recognize it for what it is. I say to him, "Bring me the book with the blue binding." It seems at least plausible to say that I referred to a rock. One might put the matter this way. Saying "the book" while merely thinking "the rock" does not constitute referring to the rock, but neither does it constitute having the intention to refer to the rock. What MacKay has ignored is the fact that the intention to refer to something in using a definite description is a complex intention involving expectations regarding one's audience. When a speaker uses a definite description referentially he intends his audience to take the description as characterizing what it is he wants to talk about. In so doing he hopes that they will successfully recognize what that is. The content of the description is clearly relevant to this intention and not something the speaker can ignore. Now if we choose to characterize the situation in which the speaker genuinely has such an intention with respect to an object, his audience, and a description, but where the description chosen fails to fit the object, as a situation in which the speaker referred to the object, no dire consequences ensue.[12]

The role of the content of a definite description used to refer comes out in another way. Suppose that two friends have a private joke about a certain book; reading it is such heavy going that they call it "the rock." One of them might say to the other, "Bring me the rock" and in doing so refer to that book. But this would not be a *definite description* used referentially. The expression "the rock" is being used rather like a name. The standard meaning of "rock" has no more than historical connection with its use here in referring to something. The two friends might even have forgotten how it came about that they call this book "the rock." In the same way it may be possible to imagine some private joke or other background that makes it suitable for a speaker using the phrase "the square root of two" to refer to a book. But it seems to me impossible to imagine a speaker to use this phrase in its standard meaning as a definite description used referentially. The reason is that I cannot conceive of the set of beliefs that would allow a speaker to suppose that this description was a means to fulfilling the intention of making it known to his audience what he is talking about via the content of the description. I can imagine a speaker mistaking a book for a rock or believing that his audience will, but I cannot imagine someone mistaking a book for the square root of two.

I have hoped to make two points in reply to MacKay. The first is that the distinction between two uses of definite descriptions can be drawn as easily in the terminology MacKay prefers as in that I used. Secondly, the dire consequences of adopting my way of talking about referring that MacKay foresees really do not materialize.

NOTES

1. I am indebted to Professor David Sachs for reading an earlier draft and making several valuable suggestions for improvement.
2. Alfred F. MacKay, "Mr. Donnellan and Humpty Dumpty on Referring," *Philosophical Review*, this issue, pp. 197–202.

3. "Reference and Definite Descriptions," *Philosophical Review*, LXXV (1966), 281–304.
4. *Philosophical Review*, LXVI (1957), 377–88.
5. Strawson thought Russell's theory of definite descriptions would have difficulty accounting for this fact, since on Russell's view a statement such as "The table is covered with books" would be literally false so long as there is more than one table in the world. Without considering the two uses of definite descriptions, the reply that one is inclined to make on Russell's behalf is that in the loose way of everyday speech the context is relied upon to supply further qualifications on the description to make it unique. This seems a plausible reply when considering attributive uses. Someone says, "The next President will be a dove on Vietnam," and context easily supplies the implicit "of the United States." But where one has a very "indefinite" definite description, with many things in the world satisfying the actual description, the reply is not so plausible. These are commonly, I believe, referential uses. A speaker wants to refer to some object and uses an "indefinite" definite description. Asked to make his description more precise, he may have to think about how best to do it. Several further descriptions may come to mind, not all of which are actually correct. Which, then, shall we say is the full but implicit one? Once we see the function of a referential description, however, we need not suppose that there is any one description recoverable from the speech act that is supposed uniquely to apply to the object referred to. The audience may through the partial description and various clues and cues know to what the speaker refers without being in possession of a description that uniquely fits it and which was implicit all along in the speaker's speech act. We can, I would suggest, view Russell's theory as a theory of attributive definite descriptions against which examples drawn from referential uses are not relevant.
6. This last feature is not independent of the first three. It is implicit in my use of "*e*." It should be noted that I allow here (and strictly should throughout) for the possibility of a referential use without a referent. This would occur when no entity can be correctly identified as "what the speaker meant to be talking about," although the speaker intended that there should be. This "failure of reference" will not come about simply because nothing is φ or because more than one thing is φ and, moreover, could happen when there is a unique φ. Thus it lends no support to MacKay's view. Exactly when it will happen could be specified only after an analysis of the criteria for deciding what entity it is to which a speaker is referring, an analysis I have not tried to give here or in the original paper.
7. For this reason it would be rather unhelpful to try to give an *analysis* of referring utilizing this expression. For example, in one use of the expression, a speaker can be talking about something although he uses no expression to refer to it. (The Secretary of State was talking about Vietnam when he said, "We must honor our commitment.") The real job of analysis would come when we tried to specify the sense of "what the speaker was talking about" we meant.

8. The speaker could lose his bet even if Smith drove a turbine-powered car and he could win it even if Smith did not.
9. Not all of my examples could be considered "near misses"—e.g., the example of misdescribing Jones as "Smith's murderer" (p. 286) when he is innocent, or of referring to a rock as "the man carrying a walking stick" (p. 296).
10. The exact connection is probably complicated and I have, I think, oversimplified it in what follows. What we can do with a certain intention not only depends upon expectations, but also upon the possibility of other means of accomplishing the same end and upon incentives. A man in the water from a sinking ship might move his arms with the intention of swimming a hundred miles to shore, if that is the only hope, even though he has no rational expectation of doing it. But is it open to an ordinary man at the beach to strike out with that intention?
11. In "Meaning," *op. cit.*
12. The situation might be summed up through an analogy. Imagine the following game of "describing." A player chooses some object and attempts to describe it. His purpose is to get a description that allows the other players to recognize the object he has chosen. Sometimes, however, a player's description will fail to characterize the object correctly. Given enough imagination we can even envisage the situation in which the object is a book and the description is "a rock." When a player grossly misses in this way, should we say that he has not described the object? Or should we say that he has described it, but incorrectly? This seems to be a verbal issue. If we opt for the second way, however, we will not be forced to say that the description a player uses is *irrelevant* just because even when he chooses the wrong one, we still say that he has described the object. (We can also imagine a game analogous to the attributive use of definite descriptions. Here a player does not first choose an object to describe. Rather he gives a description with the aim of giving one that uniquely fits some object or other.)

[3]

PROPER NAMES AND IDENTIFYING DESCRIPTIONS

I

There is an extremely plausible principle about proper names that many philosophers up to the present have either assumed or argued for.* I will call it the 'principle of identifying descriptions.' One illustration of it is in this passage from Strawson's *Individuals*:

> ... it is no good using a name for a particular unless one knows who or what is referred to by the use of the name. A name is worthless without a backing of descriptions which can be produced on demand to explain the application.[1]

The "backing of descriptions" Strawson speaks of supposedly functions as the criterion for identifying the referent of a name, if it has one, or, alternatively, for deciding that there is no referent. If I say, for example, 'Homer is my favorite poet,' then, roughly speaking, the descriptions I could supply in answer to the question, 'Who is

First published in *Synthese*, 1970, **21**: 335–58.

Homer?' provide the 'backing of descriptions.' And these in turn either pick out a single individual as the referent of the name (as it occurs in my utterance) in virtue of his fitting these descriptions or make it true that there is no referent—that Homer did not exist.

While this initial statement of the principle needs refinement and the acknowledgement of variants, it seems at first sight almost indisputable that some such principle governs the referential function of proper names. Must not a user of a proper name know to whom or what he is referring? And what can this knowledge consist in if not the ability to describe the referent uniquely?

Nevertheless, I believe the principle to be false. In the first sections of the paper I will state the principle more precisely and fill in some of the details of how it would have to operate. The exercise of trying to make it more precise and giving various needed qualifications is enough, I think, to rob it of some of its initial attractiveness. I will then, however, meet it head-on by means of counter-examples. I will argue that (a) a proper name may have a referent even though the conditions laid down by the principle are not satisfied and (b) where the conditions are satisfied, the object that ought to be the referent according to the principle need not be the true referent. In the course of this I will suggest certain positive things about how the referent of a name is determined, though these will not amount to an alternative principle.

II

What I call the 'principle of identifying descriptions' should not be thought of as expressing the thesis that proper names have a sense (or meaning or connotation). (That thesis, I think, suffers in any case from vagueness about what is to count as showing that an expression has a sense.) Anyone who holds that proper names have a sense almost certainly subscribes to the principle, but the converse is doubtful. In his influential paper, 'Proper Names,'[2] John Searle begins with the question, 'Do proper names have senses?' and he ends by saying that in a sense they do and in a sense they do not. Searle, however, though he would not without heavy qualification ascribe senses to proper names, is one of the prime examples of a philosopher who defends the principle I have in mind. In this he is in company with Frege who would have no reluctance in talking about the sense of a proper name.

The simplest application of the principle, to be sure, can be found in the view of someone such as Russell who holds that proper names are concealed definite descriptions. Russell says, "... the name 'Romulus' is not really a name [that is, in the 'narrow logical sense'] but a sort of truncated description. It stands for a person who did such-and-such things, who killed Remus, and founded Rome, and so on."[3] And again, "When I say, e.g., 'Homer existed,' I am meaning by 'Homer' some description, say 'the author of the Homeric Poems' ..."[4] Russell associates with the use of a name some definite description for which the name is a simple substitute—the same proposition would be expressed by a sentence containing the name as by the sentence formed from it by substituting the associated description for the name.

This tight connection between proper names and definite descriptions was rightly challenged by Searle in 'Proper Names.' Yet Searle still retains the backing of descriptions and these serve, as they would also for Russell, as criteria for identifying the referent, albeit in a looser and more complicated manner:

> Suppose we ask the users of the name "Aristotle" to state what they regard as certain essential and established facts about him. Their answers would be a set of uniquely referring descriptive statements. Now what I am arguing is that the descriptive force of "This is Aristotle" is to assert that a sufficient but so far unspecified number of these statements are true of this object.[5]

Without doubt this departs significantly from Russell's simplistic view. It allows for (what surely we should allow for) the possibility, for example, of discovering that Aristotle was not the teacher of Alexander the Great without having to deny Aristotle's existence, which would be impossible on Russell's view if that description was part of the associated description for our use of 'Aristotle.' Only a 'sufficient number' of the things we believe about Aristotle need be true of some individual for him to be Aristotle.

But the flexibility introduced is limited. Vague and indeterminate as we may leave the notion of 'sufficient number,' behind our use of a name a set of descriptions still operates to determine the referent. The formulation of the principle of identifying descriptions I shall give will allow both for Searle's looser and Russell's tighter connection between names and descriptions.

I should like to make one more general comment about the issue I am concerned with. The importance of the principle in question is not confined to a narrow issue about how proper names refer. It also has a bearing on the general problem of reference. For proper names constitute something like a test case for theories of reference. A peculiar feature of the situation is that two classical but opposing paradigms for referring expressions can both lead one to adopt the same theory about proper names. The model referring expression has been for many philosophers of language, I believe, a definite description (used 'attributively' in the terminology I used elsewhere).[6] An object is referred to in virtue of possessing uniquely the properties mentioned in the definite description. It is not hard to see how this standard leads to adopting the principle of identifying descriptions for proper names. Proper names are referring expressions, yet on the surface fail to exhibit any descriptive content. Given definite descriptions as the paradigm, one is forced to look under the surface (which amounts to looking into the user(s) of the name) for the 'backing of descriptions' that must be there.

The major alternative to a definite description as the paradigm of a referring expression is represented by Russell's and Wittgenstein's (in the *Tractatus*) notion of a name in the 'narrow logical sense.' Ordinary names, of course, are not names at all in this sense; they cannot meet the austere requirements of referring in some mysterious, unanalyzable and absolutely direct way to their referents. And given this notion of 'genuine' names, Russell adduces very good reasons why no such ordinary name as 'Homer' or 'Aristotle' can be a genuine name. But some account has to be given of how ordinary names function. Russell saw no alternative but to treat them as concealed definite descriptions, what they name, if anything, being whatever is denoted by the concealed description. (Had he thought of Searle's perhaps more sophisticated view, there seems no reason why he should not have adopted that for 'ordinary' proper names.)

Strangely enough, then, two antagonistic models of what a genuine referring expression is like lead their proponents to the principle of identifying descriptions. Demonstrating that that principle is mistaken would not irrevocably discredit either model, but it would, I think, take away much of the motivation for adopting either. Ordinary proper names may not have as much claim to being genuine referring expressions as Russell's names 'in the strict logical sense' (could we but understand what those are and discover some of them), but as against definite descriptions it is hard to see how they could come out second best. If their mode of functioning, however, is not captured by the principle of identifying descriptions, if, that is, they do not name in much the same way a definite description denotes,[7] then can definite descriptions possibly be model referring expressions?

And on the other side, if ordinary proper names are neither names 'in the strict logical sense,' as they surely are not, nor concealed descriptions, then some other relationship will have to be recognized as holding between some singular expressions and what they stand for. In that case, much of the reason for supposing that there are such things as names 'in the strict logical sense' will be gone. For it is clear from Russell's writings, at least, that these are introduced in part because he felt that definite descriptions not *really* being referring expressions (but only denoting expressions), some other sort of expression must serve the purpose of allowing us to talk directly about things in the world. If (ordinary) proper names do not function via the relationship of denoting nor through whatever relationship Russell's names are supposed to enjoy, then perhaps the way they do function represents the alternative Russell was seeking.[8]

III

The principle of identifying descriptions is a two-stage thesis, the second stage depending upon the first. It states, in the first place, that (with some qualifications to be noted later) the user(s) of a proper name must be able to supply a set of, as I shall call them, 'non-question-begging' descriptions in answer to the question, 'To whom (or what) does the name refer?' The important qualifier, 'non-question-begging,' I will explain later.[9] I will call these descriptions that speakers supposedly must be able to supply 'the set of identifying descriptions.'

Secondly, the principle states that the referent of a proper name (as used by a speaker in some particular utterance), if there is one, is that object that uniquely fits a 'sufficient' number of the descriptions in the set of identifying descriptions. As a corollary, when no entity (or more than one) satisfies this condition, the name has no referent and a negative existential statement expressible by a sentence of the form '*N* does not exist' (where '*N*' is the name in question) will be true.

I have tried to state the principle so as to make it possible for alternative positions still to embody it. I should like to show that we ought not to accept *any* of the versions of it to be found in the literature. Thus, for reasons that will emerge, I leave it open in the first part whether the set of identifying descriptions is to be formed from what *each* speaker can supply or from what speakers collectively supply. In the second part, the 'sufficient number' of descriptions that an object must satisfy to be the referent might be *all* of them, as in Russell's view, or some *indeterminate number* of them, as in Searle's.

The counter-examples I later give are directed against the second part of the principle; they are designed to show that *even if* the user(s) of a name must be able to supply a set of identifying descriptions, as laid down by the first part, these descriptions do not provide necessary and sufficient conditions for what shall count as the referent. But the first part of the principle is not without difficulties. To strengthen my case against the principle I want first to point out some of these while formulating some of the needed qualifications to the principle as I have just stated it.

IV

There are two views on the source of the set of identifying descriptions that supposedly must back up the use of a proper name.

We find in Russell and Frege[10] the idea that different speakers who use the same name in an otherwise identical propositional context will most likely not express the same proposition (or thought, in Frege's terminology). This happens because very probably they do not associate with the name the same set of descriptions. The propositions might have different truth-values, because the speakers, with different sets of identifying descriptions, may be referring to different things.[11] Russell and Frege, in other words, look to the individual speaker for the set of identifying descriptions.

In contrast, Searle tells us that the set of identifying descriptions is formed from the descriptions users of the name give of what they refer to. And Strawson, in discussing this question,[12] imagines a situation in which a name is used by a group in which each member "knows some distinguishing fact or facts, not necessarily the same ones, about Socrates, facts which each is prepared to cite to indicate whom he now means or understands, by 'Socrates.'" He then suggests that we form a "composite description incorporating the most frequently mentioned facts" and continues, "Now it would be too much to say that the success of term-introduction within the group by means of the name requires that there should exist just one person of whom all the propositions in the composite description are true. But it would not be too much to say that it requires that there should exist one and only one person of whom some reasonable proportion of these propositions is true."[13] Given this difference of opinion, I allowed for alternatives in the statement of the principle.

Both means of determining the set of identifying descriptions contain difficulties. To take the Russell-Frege view first, it seems to me, though evidently not to them, absurd to suppose that a beginning student of philosophy, who has learned a few things about Aristotle, and his teacher, who knows a great deal, express different propositions when each says 'Aristotle was the teacher of Alexander.' Even if this can be swallowed, there are very unpleasant consequences. Given the second part of the principle of identifying descriptions the student and teacher possess different criteria for identifying Aristotle and even for establishing his existence. For the student Aristotle would be a person satisfying (substantially) some fairly small number of descriptions; for the scholar of philosophy a much larger number would determine the existence and identity of Aristotle. This means that if each affirms Aristotle's existence there is the theoretical possibility, at least, that one is correct and the other wrong. Yet suppose that the smaller supply of descriptions available to the student turns out generally to be incorrect (we can imagine him to be unfortunate enough to have been told mostly things about Aristotle that historians of Greek philosophy are mistaken about). Would he really be in error in saying that Aristotle existed? Should we say to him, if we uncover the errors, 'Your Aristotle doesn't exist, though Professor Smith's does.'?

Worse still, suppose that the few things the student has 'learned' about Aristotle are not only not true of the individual his teacher refers to, but turn out substantially to be true of, say, Plato. He has been told, perhaps, that Aristotle wrote the *Metaphysics* when, in fact, Plato wrote it and Aristotle cribbed it, etc. Should we say that he has all along been referring to Plato, though his teacher, for whom these few descriptions are not the only source of criteria for what the referent is, continues to refer to Aristotle? The principle of identifying descriptions seems to lead to that result when interpreted in this way.

The more liberal view that utilizes descriptions suppliable by users of the name, in the plural, is not in much better shape. In the first place, what group of speakers is to form the reference set from which the 'composite description' is to be drawn? Searle speaks of properties 'commonly' attributed to Aristotle. Commonly attributed by whom? By contemporary speakers? One thing seems certain: the speakers in question cannot be *all* those who have ever used the name 'Aristotle' to refer to Aristotle. Aside from the appearance, at least, of circularity, none of us would likely ever be in a position to know what properties that group would attribute to Aristotle. Childhood friends of Aristotle, who did not follow his subsequent career, would have a quite different set of descriptions of him from ours. I doubt that we shall ever know what those were. Using this *total* class of those who have ever spoken of Aristotle is a practical impossibility and can hardly form the basis for our use. (It would also seem to do violence to the motivation behind the principle of identifying descriptions—that users of a name should be able to supply criteria for identifying the referent.)

On the other hand, to limit the group of speakers whose descriptions will generate the 'composite description' to, say, those at a particular time yields consequences similar to those of the Russell-Frege view. Different times and ages might have different beliefs about Aristotle. And in conjunction with the second part of the principle of identifying descriptions it would be possible that the affirmation that Aristotle existed should have different truth-values from one time to another. Or, because of the particular beliefs they held, we could imagine that the people of one age, unknown to any of us, referred to Plato when they used the name 'Aristotle.' On the Frege-Russell view any two people using the same sentence containing the name 'Aristotle' and believing that they are referring to the same person, etc., very likely do not express the same proposition. The more liberal view only expands this possibility to different groups of people.

V

The first part of the principle of identifying descriptions tells us that users of a name must be in a position to supply a set of identifying descriptions. (For the sake of argument I will at times allow that this is so, although what positive remarks I make will imply that there is no necessity involved.) How are we to understand this? Strawson says, "...When I speak of 'preparedness to substitute a description for a name,' this requirement must not be taken too literally. It is not required that people be very ready articulators of what they know."[14] I think he is surely right to allow us this latitude. Small children and even adults often use names without literally being able to describe the referent in sufficient detail to guarantee unique identification.

I imagine the reason philosophers who have discussed proper names so often use historical figures such as Aristotle, Homer, etc. is just that these names are introduced into our vocabulary via descriptions of facts about their bearers and most of us are prepared to give something like uniquely denoting descriptions. But it is less clear that we are ready to describe our friends, people we have met here and there, or even public figures of our times whose images have not yet been crystalized into a few memorable attributes. At the very least it would be an effort to insure that a description of someone we know fairly well and whose name we use often is both accurate and unique. The first part of the principle, then, seems to require of us a high level of ability—unless what counts as having the ability is very broad indeed. (Even though it is hardly like being able to describe the referent, the ability to *point* to the referent is usually included as if it were simply a variant.)

Construe it as broadly as you will, is there really a requirement that the user of a name be able to identify by description (or even by pointing) what the name refers to? The following example, which anticipates a bit some later results, may cast doubt on this. Suppose a child is gotten up from sleep at a party and introduced to someone as 'Tom,' who then says a few words to the child. Later the child says to his parents, "Tom is a nice man." The only thing he can say about 'Tom' is that Tom was at a party. Moreover, he is unable to recognize anyone as 'Tom' on subsequent occasions. His parents give lots of parties and they have numerous friends named 'Tom.' The case could be built up, I think, so that nothing the child possesses in the way of descriptions, dispositions to recognize, serves to pick out in the standard way anybody uniquely. That is, we cannot go by the denotation of his descriptions nor whom he points to, if anyone, etc. Does this mean that there is no person to whom he was referring? It seems to me that his parents might perfectly well conjecture about the matter and come up with a reasonable argument showing that the child was talking about this person rather than that. For example, they might reason as follows: "He's met several people named 'Tom' at recent parties, but only Tom Brown did something that might make him say, 'Tom is a nice man.' Of course, Tom Brown isn't nice and he was just indulging in his usual sarcasm when he told him, 'You have a nice pair of parents,' but the sarcasm wouldn't have registered."[15]

If this is a reasonable example, it seems the question of what a speaker referred to by using a name is not foreclosed by his inability to describe or even to recognize or point to the referent. The reasoning of the parents in this example is not aimed at finding out what descriptions the child could give, if only he were able to articulate them. I used a child in the example to sharpen the picture of someone with no descriptions or other means of identifying the referent uniquely; but adults also sometimes conjecture about other adults concerning what person they were referring to in using a name. Is it beyond doubt that in such instances the inquiry must ultimately be concerned with what descriptions the user of the name could supply? The examples later on will challenge this, yet even now examples such as the one I have given seem to me to make the requirement that every use of a name have behind it a backing of descriptions highly suspicious (even without relying on what appears to me beyond question, that no one has yet given a clear account of what the ability to describe a referent amounts to).

VI

Before turning to counter-examples one more preliminary issue should be settled. In stating the principle of identifying descriptions, I inserted the condition that the descriptions that 'back up' the use of a name should not be 'question-begging.' The qualification has vital significance because there are certain descriptions that a user of a name (providing he can articulate them) could always provide and which would always denote the referent of the name uniquely (providing there is one). No argument could be devised to show that the referent of a name need not be denoted by these descriptions. At the same time anyone who subscribes to the principle of identifying descriptions would hardly have these descriptions in mind or want to rely on them in defense of the principle. Some examples of what I shall count as 'question-begging' are the following:

(a) 'the entity I had in mind'
(b) 'the entity I referred to'
(c) 'the entity I believe to be the author of the *Metaphysics*.'

I think it is clear about (a) and (b) and only a little less so about (c) that if descriptions such as these are included in the 'backing of descriptions' the principle would become uninteresting.

Strawson, in fact, explicitly excludes descriptions such as (a): "[the speaker] cannot, for himself, distinguish the particular which he has in mind by the fact that it is the one he has in mind. So, there must be some description he could give, which need not be the description he does give, which applies uniquely to the one he has in mind and does not include the phrase, 'the one he has in mind.' "[16] Although Strawson mentions a particular description, it is certain that he would exclude from consideration similar ones. In particular, (b) above surely would not count for him. The point of the 'backing of descriptions' is to explain how an object gets referred to by a proper name. Descriptions that fit the referent simply in virtue of the fact that the speaker did, in fact, refer to it or had it in mind as the object he meant to refer to are question-begging in answer to the question, 'who (or what) did you refer to?' in the same way that 'What I have in my hand' would be question-begging in answer to the question, 'What are you holding in your hand?'

It is only a little bit less obvious that descriptions of the form, 'the object I believe to be ϕ,' such as (c) above, must likewise be excluded from the set of identifying descriptions.

Call descriptions such as 'the author of the *Metaphysics*' *primary* descriptions; call those such as 'the man I believed to be the author of the *Metaphysics*' *secondary* descriptions. Suppose that all primary descriptions the user(s) of a name can supply are false of everything. The backing of secondary descriptions would be useless in the same way that 'the object I had in mind' would be. For if I cannot rely on my primary descriptions to pick out uniquely what I refer to, trying to identify the referent via a description of the form 'the one I believed to be (though it is not) ϕ' would amount to no more than trying to identify *the object I had in mind* when I held that belief.

In what follows, then, I will count what I have called 'secondary' descriptions as question-begging.

VII

In the next sections I construct counter-examples to the principle of identifying descriptions. To do this I must show that there are possible situations in which the referent of a name does not satisfy the conditions the principle lays down or situations in which an entity satisfying those conditions is not the referent. The principle tells us that the referent of a name, if there is one, is that entity that fits some sufficient number of a certain set of descriptions, namely the set suppliable by the user(s) of the name. It is important to note that in denying this, one need not deny that there are some constraints on what the referent of a name may be—*some* description which it must fit. But this is only to allow that there may be a 'backing of descriptions' that serve as *necessary* conditions, while the principle tells us that such a backing of descriptions also serves as sufficient conditions.

Thus, I should want to argue, for example, that *theoretically* Aristotle might turn out to be a person who did *not* write the *Metaphysics*, was *not* the teacher of Alexander, etc.; that is to say, a person who does fit 'a sufficient number' of the descriptions we, as users of the name, would now supply. But I need not argue that even theoretically he could turn out to be, say, a fishmonger living in Hoboken or Plato's dog (although in incautious moments I am inclined to believe in even this outlandish theoretical possibility). If anyone wants to maintain that our use of the name is such that being a human being or not living in modern times, etc. are *necessary* for being the referent of the name, I have no objection here to offer against a 'backing of descriptions' in that weaker sense. Such an attenuated backing would not *uniquely* identify the referent.

A word about the nature of the counter-examples is required, because they will undoubtedly seem artificial and possibly taken on their own not wholly convincing. Their artificiality is in part forced on me by the fact that I want to question not only the simple view of, say, Russell that sees a name as a simple substitute for a description, but also the looser and vaguer view of Searle and Strawson. The latter, however, uses the notion of an ill-defined 'sufficient' number of descriptions. Since the notion of 'sufficient' is ill-defined, it is necessary to invent examples in which, for instance, the referent of a name fits *no* description which is both unique to it and available to the speaker (other than 'question-begging' descriptions). Otherwise, a defender of the view might take refuge in those descriptions. To make sure that there are no remaining contaminating descriptions, the examples have to be fairly extreme ones in which the user(s) of a name are radically deceived about the properties of what they are talking about.

But if these 'pure' examples are in order in everything except their artificiality, then the fact that I do not tell more true-to-life stories should not be an objection. For however vague 'sufficient number' is left, one thing is certain: the Searle-Strawson view cannot be that the referent of a name is any entity that fits uniquely any *one* of the descriptions suppliable by the user(s) of the name. The whole purpose of this variant (as opposed to the stronger Russell view) is to allow that we could discover, e.g., that Aristotle did not teach Alexander without having to deny Aristotle's existence or that *someone else* was the teacher of Alexander. But if any *one* of the descriptions in the set of identifying descriptions counts always as 'sufficient,' there will be an overwhelming number of cases in which there cannot be a unique referent for a name we use—all those instances in which we ascribe to the referent two or more properties which in fact are unique properties of more than one person.

VIII

The first counter-example is the most artificial (but perhaps the most pure). It is a situation in which a speaker uses a name to refer to something though what is referred to is not picked out uniquely by the descriptions available to the speaker. As well, there is something the speaker's descriptions denote uniquely, but that is not the referent.

Imagine the following circumstances: Perhaps in an experiment by psychologists interested in perception a subject is seated before a screen of uniform color and large enough to entirely fill his visual field. On the screen are painted two squares of identical size and color, one directly above the other. The subject knows nothing of the history of the squares—whether one was painted before the other, etc. Nor does he know anything about their future. He is asked to give names to the squares[17] and to say on what basis he assigns the names. With one complication to be noted later, it seems that the only way in which he can distinguish the squares through description is by their relative positions. So he might respond that he will call the top square 'alpha' and the bottom square 'beta.'

The catch in the example is this: unknown to the subject, he has been fitted with spectacles that invert his visual field. Thus, the square he sees as apparently on top is really on the bottom and *vice versa*. Having now two names to work with we can imagine the subject using one of them to say something about one of the squares. Suppose he comes to believe (whether erroneously or not doesn't matter) that one of the squares has changed color. He might report, 'Alpha is now a different color.' But which square is he referring to? He would describe alpha as the square on top. And if this is the only uniquely identifying description at his command then according to the principle I am attacking, he would have referred to the square that is on top. But given our knowledge of the presence and effect of the inverting spectacles and the ignorance of the subject about that, it seems clear that we should take him as referring to, not the square on top, but the one that seems to him erroneously to be on top—the one on the bottom. We know why he describes 'alpha' the way he does; we expect changes in the square on the bottom to elicit from him reports of changes in alpha, etc. I think it would be altogether right to say that although *he* does not know it, he is talking about the square on the bottom even though he would *describe* it as 'the square on top.' If this is right, we seem to have a case in which the speaker's descriptions of what he is referring to when he uses a name do not yield the true referent so long as we stick to what is denoted by the descriptions he gives. The referent is something different and the thing actually denoted is not the referent.

This counter-example to the principle of identifying descriptions depends upon the supposition that the subject's only description that could serve to pick out the referent uniquely is the one in terms of relative position. But it must be admitted that I have so far neglected a description of alpha that he could supply, that is not question-begging, and that would in fact uniquely identify alpha despite the operation of the glasses. The subject could describe alpha as, 'the square that *appears* to me to be on top.' We must take 'appears' here in its phenomenological sense. If 'that appears to me to be on top' means 'that I believe to be on top' we would have a question-begging description. But in its phenomenological sense, alpha is the one that *appears* to him to be on top and, indeed, it is just because the square on the bottom is the one that appears to him to be on top that it is the referent of 'alpha.'

There is more than one way to modify the example in order to take care of this objection to it, but an easy way is by having the subject use the name 'alpha' a bit later having forgotten how alpha appeared to him, but recalling the position he took it really to have. Of course in our example as presented the subject would have no reason to suppose that there might be a discrepancy between the actual position of alpha and what position it appeared to him to have and so long as he remembered it as being the one on top, he would presumably say that that was also the way it appeared to him. What is needed is something to make him doubt that his recollection of what position he took alpha to have is an accurate guide to how it appeared to him.

Suppose then that our subject is an old hand at experiments of this sort and knows that inverting lenses are sometimes put into the spectacles he wears. Erroneously he believes he has a method of detecting when this happens. He goes through the experiment as previously described but with the mistaken belief that his spectacles have not been tampered with and that the squares have the position they appear to him to have. Later on he makes some statement such as, 'Alpha changed color at one point.' But while he remembers his judgment that alpha was the top square (and has absolute confidence in it), he cannot remember how alpha appeared to him at the time nor whether he had based his judgment on the assumption that his visual field was inverted or not. The subject's set of identifying descriptions thus no longer contains the *appearance* description and only the erroneous description of alpha as being the square on top remains as a uniquely identifying description.

IX

If the preceding counter-example was persuasive, then it will also suggest something positive. Its moral might be put this way: When a person describes something, as when he describes what he is referring to, *we* are not limited to looking for something that fits his descriptions uniquely (or fits them better than anything else). We can also ask ourselves, 'What thing would he *judge* to fit those descriptions, even if it does not really do so?' That question will utilize his descriptions, but will not be decided on the rigid basis of what is denoted, if anything, uniquely by them. In this particular example the influence of inverting spectacles was a deciding factor. We had to know *both* how he described the referent and, what he did not know, that the spectacles would influence his descriptions in a certain way. The role of his set of 'identifying descriptions' in determining the referent of his use of a name is not that which the principle of identifying descriptions gives it. It had its part, but the question asked about it was different: 'What do these descriptions denote uniquely (or best)?' vs. 'Why should he describe the referent in that way?'

The next counter-example[18] provides a somewhat different insight into how proper names function.

A student meets a man he takes to be the famous philosopher, J. L. Aston-Martin. Previously, the student has read some of the philosopher's works and so has at his command descriptions such as, "the author of 'Other Bodies'" and "the leading expounder of the theory of egocentric pluralism." The meeting takes place at a party and the student engages the man in a somewhat lengthy conversation, much of it given over, it turns out, to trying to name cities over 100,000 in population in descending order of altitude above sea level. In fact, however, although the student never suspects it, the man at the party is not the famous philosopher, but someone who leads the student to have that impression. (We can even imagine that by coincidence he has the same name.)

Imagine, then, a subsequent conversation with his friends in which the student relates what happened at the party. He might begin by saying, "Last night I met J. L. Aston-Martin and talked to him for almost an hour." To whom does he refer at this point? I strongly believe the answer should be, 'to the famous philosopher,' and not, 'to the man he met at the party.' What the student says is simply false; a friend 'in the know' would be justified in replying that he did not meet J. L. Aston-Martin, but someone who had the same name and was no more a philosopher than Milton Berle.

Suppose, however, that the audience contains no such doubting Thomases, and that the rest of the party was of sufficient interest to generate several more stories about what went on. The student might use the name 'J. L. Aston-Martin,' as it were, incidently. For example: "... and then Robinson tripped over Aston-Martin's feet and fell flat on his face" or "I was almost the last to leave—only Aston-Martin and Robinson, who was still out cold, were left."

In these subsequent utterances to whom was the speaker referring in using the name, 'Aston-Martin'? My inclination is to say that here it was to the man he met at the party and not to the famous philosopher. Perhaps the difference lies in the fact that in the initial utterance the speaker's remark would only have a point if he was referring to the famous philosopher, while in the later utterances it is more natural to take him to be referring to the man at the party, since what happened there is the whole point.[19]

If in such examples as this there are *two* references made (or even if there is a strong inclination to say that there are) this is something unaccounted for by the principle of identifying descriptions.

To see this we need only ask what the student's set of identifying descriptions consists in each time he uses the name, first when he claims to have met Aston-Martin and later when he recounts events at the party that incidently involve the man he met there. In both cases the set of identifying descriptions would be the same. It will include, first of all, those descriptions of Aston-Martin he would have given prior to the party—the author of certain works, propounder of certain doctrines, etc. In addition, it would now contain various descriptions derived from meeting the spurious famous man at the party—the man who played the game about cities, whose feet Robinson tripped over, etc.

The full set of descriptions, available to him when he later talks about the party, would be the same whether he was asked, 'Who is Aston-Martin?' at the outset when he claims to have met Aston-Martin at the party or later on when the name occurs in recounting other events involving the man met at the party. *We* may say that the referent changes during the course of his conversation, but the speaker would not. And his full account, i.e. all the descriptions at his command, of who it is he refers to would remain the same. It would contain, for example, both "the author of 'Other Bodies'" and "the man I talked to at the party about cities."

This result, however, is inconsistent with the principle of identifying descriptions. On that principle, the *same* set of identifying descriptions can determine at most *one* referent. But in this example we seem to have two referents and only one set of identifying descriptions.

We extracted from the first counter-example the idea that the question we should ask is, 'What would the user(s) of the name describe in this way?' rather than, 'What (substantially) fits the descriptions they give?' Though these questions may usually have the same answer, the counter-example showed that they need not.

The present example, however, shows that even this distinction is not enough. It would do no good to ask about his set of identifying descriptions, 'Who would the speaker describe that way?' In the example the same set of identifying descriptions is related to two different referents. It seems then that the ultimate question is rather, 'What would the speaker describe in this way on this occasion?' where 'describe in this way' does not refer to his set of identifying descriptions, but to the predicate he ascribes to the referent; e.g., in the example, we might ask on one occasion, 'Who would he claim to have met at the party?' on another, 'Who would he want us to believe Jones tripped over at the party?' And although *his* answer, gleaned from his set of identifying descriptions, would be the same in either case, *we* may have reason to answer differently to each question.

X

It is instructive to look at the use of proper names in historical contexts if only to see why so many philosophers who discuss proper names appeal to examples of it. In general, our use of proper names for persons in history (and also those we are not personally acquainted with) is parasitic on uses of the names by other people—in conversation, written records, etc. Insofar as we possess a set of identifying descriptions in these cases they come from things said about the presumed referent by other people. My answer to the question, 'Who was Thales?' would probably derive from what I learned from my teachers or from histories of philosophy. Frequently, as in this example, one's identifying descriptions trace back through many levels of parasitic derivation. Descriptions of Thales we might give go back to what was said, using that name, by Aristotle and Herodotus. And, if Thales existed, the trail would not end there.

The history behind the use of a name may not be known to the individual using it. I may have forgotten the sources from whence I got my descriptions of Thales. Even a whole culture could lose this history. A people with an oral tradition in which names of past heroes figure would probably not be able to trace the history back to original sources. Yet, for all that, they may be telling of the exploits of real men in the past and they may possess knowledge of them and their deeds.

Yet, in such cases the history is of central importance to the question of whether a name in a particular use has a referent and, if so, what it is. The words of others, in conversation, books and documents can, like the inverting spectacles in a previous example, distort our view of what we are naming. But at the same time it can, to one who knows the facts, provide the means of uncovering the referent, if there is one.

The role of this history leading up to a present use of a name has almost always been neglected by those who accept the principle of identifying descriptions. The sort of description generally mentioned as helping to pick out, say, Thales, is such as 'the Greek philosopher who held that all is water.' Nothing is made of the fact that such descriptions are given by us derivatively. We might be pardoned if we supposed that the referent of 'Thales' is whatever ancient Greek happens to fit such descriptions uniquely, even if he should turn out to have been a hermit living so remotely that he and his doctrines have no historical connection with us at all.

But this seems clearly wrong. Suppose that Aristotle and Herodotus were either making up the story or were referring to someone who neither did the things they said he did nor held the doctrines they attributed to him. Suppose further, however, that fortuitously their descriptions fitted uniquely someone they had never heard about and who was not referred to by any authors known to us. Such a person, even if he was the only ancient to hold that all is water, to fall in a well while contemplating the stars, etc., is not 'our' Thales.

Or, to take the other possible outcome according to the principle of identifying descriptions, suppose no one to have held the ridiculous doctrine that all is water, but that Aristotle and Herodotus were referring to a real person—a real person who was not a philosopher, but a well-digger with a reputation for saying wise things and who once exclaimed, "I wish everything were water so I wouldn't have to dig these damned wells." What is the situation then regarding our histories of philosophy? Have they mentioned a non-existent person or have they mentioned someone who existed but who did not have the properties they attribute to him? My inclination is to say the latter. Yet ignoring the history of these uses of the name 'Thales,' the principle of identifying descriptions would tell us that Thales did not exist. But then to whom were Aristotle and Herodotus referring? Surely we cannot conclude, 'to no one.' It seems to me to make sense that we should discover that Thales was after all a well-digger and that Aristotle and Herodotus were deceived about what he did. That would not make sense, however, if we are forced to conclude in such a case that he did not exist. That is, if we neglect the fact that there is a history behind our use of the name 'Thales' or 'Aristotle' and concentrate only upon the descriptions we would supply about their life, their works and deeds, it is possible that our descriptions are substantially wrong without the consequence being that we have not been referring to any existent person.

It is significant that descriptions of the form '*N* was referred to by *A*' should assume central importance in the case of uses of names that are parasitic on their use by others. Not only does the principle of identifying descriptions, as it has usually been defended, fail to prepare us for the special role of one type of description, but we now see that there is a quite ordinary sense in which a person might be ignorant of the nature of the entity he has referred to in using a name. While I do not want to classify descriptions of this form as 'question-begging' in the way in which 'the entity *I* have in mind' is question-begging, it seems nevertheless natural to say that in knowing only that Thales was a man referred to by Aristotle and Herodotus, I'm not in a position to *describe* the man Thales; that is, there is,

I think, an ordinary use of 'describe' in which to say only 'the man referred to by Aristotle and Herodotus' is not yet to *describe* Thales. So it seems that we could be in the position of having referred to someone in using the name 'Thales,' the same person in fact referred to by Aristotle and Herodotus, although we are not in the position of being able to describe him correctly.

Nevertheless, so long as the user of a name can fall back on such a description as 'the person referred to by Aristotle,' the principle of identifying descriptions may be salvaged even if at expense of having to elevate one type of description to special status. But it is not at all clear that such descriptions will in general be available to the user of a name or that without them the failure of his other descriptions to identify the referent uniquely must mean that the name has no referent. In the case of individual people there are surely many who would, for example, identify Thales as the pre-Socratic philosopher who held that all is water, but who do not know that he was referred to by Aristotle and Herodotus. And in fact they may not know even the immediate sources of their use of the name; that, for example, Thales was referred to by Mr. Jones, their freshman philosophy instructor. In case Thales was in fact the pre-Socratic philosopher with that doctrine, such people surely know something about Thales and, in using the name, they have referred to him. But if, in fact, the attribution of this view to Thales is wrong and they are left without any descriptions that uniquely fit Thales, I do not believe it follows that they have not referred to anyone or that (in their use of the name) Thales did not exist. To be sure, they may have available to them some such description of Thales as, 'The one who is commonly believed to have been a pre-Socratic philosopher who held that all is water.' But even this may not be true. Everyone may have come to believe that Thales did not have that doctrine. One could continue along these lines, I think, to deny an individual any identifying descriptions, even of the form 'The one referred to by so-and-so' that will serve uniquely to pick out Thales, without the consequence that he has not referred to anyone.

XI

The previous examples have concentrated on individuals and the set of descriptions they could supply. But I think there is no reason to suppose that, with a bit more stretching of the imagination, the same results could not be gotten for the whole of some group in which a name is used. Thus, those who would form the 'set of identifying descriptions' from a collective effort at description seem no better off to me.

Thus, we could imagine a future time, for example, when the plays we attribute to Shakespeare are available and it is believed that Shakespeare was their author, but little else is known about him—perhaps only that he was an actor in Elizabethan times—and, in particular, nothing about the documentation we rely upon in attributing the plays to him has survived. As we now view it, the people of this future generation would be correct in saying that Shakespeare wrote *Hamlet*. But suppose in fact the Baconian hypothesis is correct—Francis Bacon wrote those plays. What should an omniscient being who sees the whole history of the affair conclude about one of these future beings saying that Shakespeare wrote *Hamlet*? (Surely not that as they use 'Shakespeare' it refers to Bacon—Bacon was not an actor and they may know a great deal about Bacon, enough to insure that he could not have been an actor.) It seems to me that the correct conclusion should be that (perhaps because we did not pay enough attention to the cryptologists who claim to find this message in the plays) we and they have made a mistake—we both believe that Shakespeare wrote the plays, though it was rather Bacon and not Shakespeare who is the Bard.

XII

As I have admitted, my counter-examples are necessarily somewhat artificial because of the vagueness of the position I want to attack. Yet, it seems to me that even artificial examples are sufficient because I take the principle of identifying descriptions to be a doctrine about how reference via proper names *must* take place. If these examples show that there are other possibilities for identifying the referent, they do their job. It is the idea that *only* a backing of descriptions identifying the referent by its fitting them (or some sufficient number of them) could serve to connect an object with a name that I question.

On the positive side my view is that what we should substitute for the question, 'What is the referent?' is 'What would the speaker be attributing that predicate to on this occasion?' Thus, in an early example, the parents of a child ask, 'Who would he say was a nice man at a party of ours?' when the child has said, 'Tom was a nice man.' *How* we answer such questions I do not have a general theory about. It seems clear to me that in some way the referent must be historically, or, we might say, causally connected to the speech act. But I do not see my way clear to saying exactly how in general that connection goes. Perhaps there is no exact theory.

The shift of question, however, seems to be important. One can explain why the principle of identifying descriptions has seemed so plausible, for example, while denying its validity. If a speaker says '*a* is ϕ,' where '*a*' is a name, and we ask, "To what would he on this occasion attribute the predicate 'ϕ'?" asking him for descriptions would *normally* be the best strategy for finding out. Generally we know numbers of correct and even uniquely identifying descriptions of the referent of names we use. So others would naturally first rely on these and look for what best fits them.

To illustrate this, we can imagine the following games: In the first a player gives a set of descriptions and the other players try to find the object in the room that best fits them. This is analogous to the role of the set of identifying descriptions in the principle I object to. In the other game the player picks out some object in the room, tries to give descriptions that characterize it uniquely and the other players attempt to discover what object he described. In the second game the problem set for the other players (the audience in the analogue) is to find out what is being described, not what best fits the descriptions. Insofar as descriptions enter into a determination of what the referent of a name is, I suggest that the second game is a better analogy. In that game, on the normal assumption that people are unlikely to be badly mistaken about the properties of an object they are describing, the other players would usually first look for an object best fitting the descriptions given. But that need not always be the best tactics. They may notice or conjecture that the circumstances are such that the describer has unintentionally *mis*-described the object, the circumstances being such as distortions in his perception, erroneous beliefs he is known to hold, etc.

One final point: I earlier questioned whether we can really expect that there must be a backing of descriptions behind the use of a proper name. Insofar as I offer an alternative to the principle of identifying descriptions, it has the merit of not requiring such a backing. If a speaker says '*a* is ϕ,' where '*a*' is a name, the question of what he referred to does not hinge on what he can supply in the way of descriptions—though what descriptions he does give, if any, can constitute an important datum. It may be possible to answer the question, "To what would he on this occasion attribute the predicate 'is ϕ'?" without any backing of descriptions.

NOTES

* I am indebted to students and colleagues for comments and suggestions, in particular Professor John Perry and Mr. Theodore Budlong. I believe also that some departure from the traditional alternatives in theories about reference and proper names is "in the air" and that views along some of the lines I take in this paper I may share with others, although the view I attack is still the dominant one. I believe that Saul Kripke has a very similar position, at least insofar as denial of the prevalent theories go. And, indeed, I think I may owe one of my counter-examples to him through a secondhand source (although I did not understand the relevance until much later). David Kaplan's paper, "Quantifying In," *Synthese* **19** (1969) 178–214, also seems to me to be in the same vein, though I am not sure I agree with a variety of details and the main purpose of the paper is not to mount an assault on theories of proper names.

1. P. F. Strawson, *Individuals*, Methuen & Co. Ltd., London, 1959, p. 20.
2. *Mind* **67** (1958) 166–173.
3. "Lectures on Logical Atomism" in *Logic and Knowledge* (ed. by Robert C. Marsh), George Allen & Unwin Ltd., London, 1956, p. 243.
4. Ibid., p. 252.
5. "Proper Names," *op. cit.*, p. 171.
6. In "Reference and Definite Descriptions," *The Philosophical Review* **75** (1966) pp. 281–304, and "Putting Humpty Dumpty Together Again," *The Philosophical Review* **77** (1968) 203–15.
7. I assume here Russell's definition of denoting, which I think makes it a well-defined relation and ought always to be kept in mind in discussions of reference so that other relations may be compared with it: An entity X is denoted by a definite description, "the ϕ," just in case X uniquely possesses the property designated by "ϕ."
8. Although I do not have space to develop it, my account of proper names in this paper seems to me to make what I called "referential" definite descriptions (as discussed in "Reference and Definite Descriptions," *op. cit.*) a close relative of proper names.
9. Below, Section VI.
10. E.g., in "The Thought: A Logical Inquiry" (translated by A. M. and Marcelle Quinton), *Mind* (1956) 289–311. Also in P. F. Strawson (ed.), *Philosophical Logic*, Oxford Readings in Philosophy, Oxford University Press, Oxford, 1967, pp. 17–38.

11. That is to say, *if* what they refer to is a function of the set of identifying descriptions each possesses. In that case there would be the logical possibility of each speaker's set picking out different objects, each possessing the properties one speaker would attribute to the referent, but not those the other would.
12. *Individuals, op. cit.*, pp. 191–92.
13. *Loc. cit.*
14. Ibid., p. 182, footnote 1.
15. The last part of the remark is there simply to indicate that the parents need not even consider what the child says to be *true*; not only does the child not have a "backing of descriptions," but the predicate in the sentence he uses need not apply. This connects up with the position suggested later in the paper.
16. *Individuals, op. cit.*, p. 182.
17. In the example as presented I have the subject of the experiment introduce the names. Nothing hinges on this. The experimenters could just as well use the names and give the subjects "identifying descriptions." Nor is there any importance in the fact that the example contains people, the experimenters, "in the know." For all that, everyone concerned might have the inverting spectacles on that I introduce.
18. The idea behind this example originated with me from a conversation with Rogers Albritton in 1966 and may derive from Saul Kripke, who has, I believe, a view about proper names not dissimilar to the one in this paper.
19. For the purpose of keeping the example within limits, I compress the two uses of the name, that I claim refer, unknown to the speaker, to two different people, into one conversation. I have sometimes, however, found it useful to make the case stronger intuitively by supposing that the person met at the party, for example, who is *not* the famous philosopher, becomes a longer term acquaintance of the speaker (who continues under the illusion that he is the famous man). In subsequent conversation, perhaps months or years later and after his friends have met the bogus philosopher, his use of the name is even more clearly a reference to the man he met at the party and whom he continues to see. Yet if he claimed to know, as in my example, J. L. Aston-Martin, in circumstances where it is clear that the point of the remark has to do with claiming to know a famous man, I still think we would suppose him to have referred to Aston-Martin, the famous philosopher, and not to man he met at the party, who later is one of his close acquaintances.

[4]

SPEAKING OF NOTHING

Russell tells us[1] in "On Denoting" to test our logical theories by their "capacity for dealing with puzzles."[2] In this paper I raise the question of how a theory of reference, one of recent origin, might handle one of the major puzzles Russell mentioned. The theory of reference that I have in mind—and one I subscribe to—I will call "the historical explanation theory." (It, or ones similar to it in important respects, has also been called the "causal theory." For various reasons, I prefer a different title.)[3]

Among a number of puzzles mentioned by Russell, two stand out as more important than the others. One is the well-known problem of identity statements with which Frege begins his article, "On Sense and Reference,"[4] the question of how a statement of the form "*a* is identical to *b*," when true, can differ in "cognitive value" from a corresponding statement of the apparently trivial form, "*a* is identical to *a*." The second puzzle is the topic of this paper. In a large number of situations speakers apparently refer to the nonexistent. The most obvious example of this is, perhaps, the use of singular terms in negative existence statements—for example, "The discoverer of the philosopher's stone does not exist" or "Robin Hood did not exist." The problem is, of course, well known and ancient in

First published in *The Philosophical Review*, 1974, **83**: 3–31.

origin: such statements seem to refer to something only to say about it that it does not exist. How can one say something about what does not exist? For a few philosophers, to be sure, these questions have led to attempts to provide the referent. But in general such attempts have been met with suspicion. Russell certainly thought it a merit of his theory of definite descriptions (and his fully developed views on singular expressions) that such apparent references to the nonexistent were explained without having to entertain the idea of referents of singular terms that are nonexistent.

Where the singular terms involved are definite descriptions, "On Denoting" provided a solution to the two puzzles mentioned that was at once a breakthrough in the treatment of these expressions and satisfying in the coherent explanation it gave. Russell's fully developed theory of singular terms, perhaps best represented in "Lectures on Logical Atomism,"[5] extends the proposed solution to ordinary proper names, for these turn out to be concealed definite descriptions. The view of "On Denoting" now could be made to cover most of the uses of singular terms in language as we actually speak it and, moreover, seemed to meet the test of solving the various puzzles about reference. But the fully developed view also introduced a category of singular expressions that were acknowledged to be rarely, if ever, found in everyday speech—what Russell called names in "the strict logical sense" or "genuine" names.

Genuine names and the motivation for giving pride of place to such exotic singular terms have special interest for the historical explanation theory, because while its treatment of ordinary singular expressions is radically different from Russell's it has some similarities to his characterization of genuine names.

The question posed, then, is how the historical explanation theory of reference can handle the puzzle that Russell's view has no difficulty with, the problem of apparent reference to the nonexistent.

I cannot in this paper plead the full case for the historical explanation theory, though I shall try to give its main features; so it may be best to consider it an exercise in the hypothetical: *if* the theory is correct what follows concerning apparent reference to the nonexistent?[6]

I. THREE KINDS OF APPARENT REFERENCE TO THE NONEXISTENT

We need to keep distinct three situations in which apparent reference to the nonexistent occurs. The differences are important in their own right, but I need to call attention to them because one kind of situation will be excluded from consideration in this paper.

I will, in the first place, distinguish what I will call "discourse about fiction" from "discourse about actuality"; and, secondly, within the latter category, the use of "predicative" statements from the use of "existence" statements.[7] What is to be excluded from consideration here is an account of discourse about fiction. (This is not, of course, to say that such an account is not in the end needed.)

Under "discourse about fiction" I mean to include those occasions on which it is a presupposition of the discourse that fictional, mythological, legendary (and so forth) persons, places, or things are under discussion. I believe, for example, that said with the right intention, the following sentences would express true propositions: "The Green Hornet's car was called 'Black Beauty,'" "Snow White lived with seven dwarves," and "To reach the underworld, one must first cross the River Styx." (By the "right intention" I mean that the speaker wishes to be taken as talking about fiction, mythology, or legend.) At the same time I also believe it is true that neither the Green Hornet, his car, Snow White, nor the River Styx exists or ever has existed. These two beliefs, however, are entirely consistent. And therein lies the puzzle: how can there be true propositions that apparently involve predicating properties of what does not exist?

Discourse about actuality carries the presupposition that the speaker is talking about people, places, or things that occur in the history of our world. A puzzle arises when the speaker is unfortunate enough to use a singular expression, intending to attribute a property to something, but fails, in his use of that expression, to refer to anything. This very likely occurred, for example, some years ago following the publication of *The Horn Papers*,[8] that purported to contain the diary of one Jacob Horn and that would, if genuine, have shed light on the colonial history of Washington County, Pennsylvania. Many people believed them to be genuine, but, on the evidence, it seems likely that they are not and that Jacob Horn did not exist. There must have been many believers, however, who made statements using the name "Jacob Horn" with the intention of predicating various properties of a historical figure. For example, someone might well have said, "Jacob Horn wrote about Augusta Town and now we know where it was located." It would have been some sort of inconsistency—exactly what kind is another question—for such a speaker then to affirm the nonexistence of Jacob Horn. This contrasts with discourse about fiction—there one can, for example, consistently deny the existence of Snow White while also stating that she enraptured a prince.[9]

The puzzle about predicative statements, as I shall call them, in discourse about actuality with a singular expression and no referent is more subtle philosophically than the puzzle about fictional discourse. There is not the same possibility of stating something true. Nor can the speaker with consistency acknowledge the nonexistence of what he speaks about. To see how statements such as those made by believers in the authenticity of *The Horn Papers* can puzzle a philosopher requires the ability to see a difficulty in how one can even speak and be *understood* when using a singular expression with no referent.

The difference between discourse about fiction and discourse about reality, it is important to keep in mind, is a matter of presuppositions about the intent of the speech act. It is not that in the one fictional characters are involved and in the other real people, places, and things. A not too well-informed person might have taken (at least the first part of) the movie *Doctor Strangelove* for a documentary. His statement, "Doctor Strangelove, the top military scientist in the United States, is a psychopath," would then be a bit of discourse about reality, even though Doctor Strangelove is, in fact, fictional. On the other hand, this very same sentence used by someone having seen the whole movie would probably be a comment on the movie, a bit of discourse about fiction.

While I will need often to consider predicative statements about actuality, the problem I want to concentrate on concerns "existence" statements—those that have either the form "*S* does not exist" or the form "*S* exists," where "*S*" is a singular expression. Negative existence statements, unlike predicative statements, are true when there is no referent for the singular expression. If I speak the truth in saying, "Jacob Horn does not exist," I would be apparently referring to what does not exist. But even more paradoxically, the truth of what I say depends directly upon the nonexistence of a referent for "Jacob Horn." Moreover, this is discourse about reality; I do not, clearly, intend to talk about a fictional character. Negative existence statements, of all those mentioned, bring apparent reference to the nonexistent into sharpest focus.

It is of some importance to mention the difference between denying the existence of something altogether and denying its present existence or its existence at some point or during some period in time. To begin with we certainly want to distinguish between

(1) Napoleon no longer exists,

and

(2) Napoleon does not and never did exist.

The first statement is both true and not an apparent reference to the nonexistent in the sense we want. (1) contains a reference to Napoleon in the same way that "Socrates was snub-nosed" contains a reference to Socrates. (1) should, it seems, be put into the class of predicative statements, despite the fact that existence is involved. On the other hand, (2) is a paradigm of the kind of statement that generates the problem of apparent reference to the nonexistent.

What shall we say, however, about a statement such as

(3) Santa Claus does not exist?

Often, I believe, it expresses a statement of the same form as (2), an absolute denial of existence, not confined to any one period in time. But suppose, for example, that someone is unsure whether Jacob Horn ever did exist, but is certain that he does not now exist. He might express this by saying, "Jacob Horn does not exist." So, perhaps, sentences of the surface form of (3) are ambiguous. But what is the other meaning that they might have? The sentence given, in the imagined circumstances, seems to me to be equivalent to

(4) Jacob Horn does not now exist.

This is neither the absolute denial of Jacob Horn's existence nor the predicative assertion that Jacob Horn no longer exists. (4), I believe, amounts to the disjunction of the two: "Either Jacob Horn does not and never did exist or he did exist and does no longer." In which case, the dichotomy illustrated by (1) and (2) is still maintained. In what follows, however, it is the absolute denial of existence that will be of concern and any examples of the form "$\mathcal{N}$ does not exist" should be construed in that way.

II. A THEORY GONE WRONG WITH INTERESTING MOTIVES—RUSSELL

Russell's theory of singular terms holds interest for the historical explanation theory, not only because of obvious oppositions on some key issues—several more recent discussions would serve that purpose[10]—but also because certain problems and issues that evidently motivated features of Russell's theory that are nowadays generally ignored or thought obviously wrong are brought to the fore once again by the historical explanation theory. I believe that much of Russell's theory has been accepted by many philosophers with the thought that there was a certain excrescence that could be ignored. Russell's views on ordinary singular terms, definite descriptions, proper names in ordinary language have wide acceptance; his addition of "genuine" names to the ranks has generally been ignored as so much metaphysical meandering. I think there is no doubt that "genuine" names, as Russell characterized them, have no place in a correct theory of reference. But from the first, in "On Denoting," Russell contrasted his account of those singular terms for which his theory provided a way out of puzzles about reference with another kind of singular term, a "genuine" name, for which he seemed to feel there was a theoretical need. But, of course, "genuine" names, if they were to be included in the general theory, could not reintroduce the same puzzles. This, I think, accounts for some of the peculiar properties attributed to "genuine" names: for example, the distinction between "knowledge by acquaintance" and "knowledge by description" that gave the result that we could only genuinely name something we are acquainted with in a very strong sense seems to have been introduced in part to make it impossible to assert negative existence statements using "genuine" names.

The reason this has interest for the historical explanation theory is that Russell's contrast, the radical difference between most singular terms in ordinary language and "genuine" names, is that the former have descriptive content and the latter do not. Given his view of singular terms with descriptive content, the puzzles about reference yield easily for them. He felt, however, some need to have singular expressions, nonetheless, that do not function in accord with his analysis of definite descriptions and ordinary proper names. The historical explanation theory denies that, for at least many uses of ordinary singular expressions, Russell's view is correct. In particular, it denies that ordinary proper names always have descriptive content. The question is, does this mean that perhaps ordinary singular expressions may fulfill the function that Russell thought only "genuine" names, with all their peculiarities, could? And, if so, how can the historical explanation view deal with the puzzles about reference?

What was the motivation for introducing "genuine" names? Russell often talks in ways that can seem nonsensical—that, for example, when a definite description such as "the author of *Waverly*" is involved, the denotation of the definite description, Scott in this case, is not a "constituent" of the proposition expressed. The implied contrast is that if "Scott" is a genuine name and were there in place of the definite description "the author of *Waverly*" then Scott would be a constituent. But it certainly sounds queer at first glance to find a flesh-and-blood person in a proposition!

Russell's analysis of statements containing definite descriptions and, by extension, ordinary proper names, shows, he believed, that such statements are not really *about,* do not really *mention,* the denotation of the description or the referent of the name. Russell emphasizes this again and again. "Genuine" names, on the other hand, can somehow perform the feat of really mentioning a particular individual. To try to put much weight on such terms as "about" would lead us, I think, into a morass. What it is for a statement to be *about* an individual, if that requires any attempt to define *aboutness,* is a question better avoided if we are ever to get on with the problem. (After all, Russell himself recognized a well-defined relationship that a statement containing a definite description can have to some particular individual—its denotation. It would be a delicate task to show either that in no sense of "about" is such a statement *about* the denotation of the definite description or that there is some clear sense of "about" in which it is not.)

But I believe we can say something useful about the reasons Russell had for talking in this way. On his theory of definite descriptions the singular expression, the definite description, is really a device that introduces quantifiers and converts what might seem at first sight a simple proposition about an individual into a general proposition. "The ϕ is ψ" expresses the same proposition as "There is a ϕ and there is at most one ϕ and all ϕ's are ψ's"; and the latter clearly would express a general proposition about the world. Ordinary proper names, of course, function on his view in the same way, since they are in reality concealed definite descriptions. Now if we contrast these singular expressions with ones, if there are any, that do not introduce quantifiers, that when put as the subject of a simple subject-predicate sentence do not make the sentence express a general proposition, then I think there is a strong temptation to say that only the second kind of singular term can be used to really mention an individual.

Russell clearly believed that there must be the possibility, at least, of singular terms that do not introduce quantifiers; that seems in large part to be his reason for believing in "genuine" names. Whether or not there is some argument that shows the necessity of such singular terms, I believe that prior to theory the natural view is that they occur often in ordinary speech. So if one says, for example, "Socrates is snub-nosed," the natural view seems to me to be that the singular expression "Socrates" is simply a device used by the speaker to pick out what he wants to talk about while the rest of the sentence expresses what property he wishes to attribute to that individual. This can be made somewhat more precise by saying, first, that the natural view is that in using such simple sentences containing singular terms we are not saying something general about the world—that is, not saying something that would be correctly analyzed with the aid of quantifiers; and, second, that in such cases the speaker could, in all probability, have said the same thing, expressed the same proposition, with the aid of other and different singular expressions, so long as they are being used to refer to the same individual. To illustrate the latter point with a different example: if, at the same moment in time, one person were to say, "Smith is happy," a second "You are happy," a third "My son is happy," and a fourth "I am happy," and if in each case the singular expression refers to the same person, then all four have expressed the same proposition, have agreed with each other.

What I see as the natural pre-theoretical view might be captured as a certain way of representing what proposition is expressed. For example, the sentence "Socrates is snub-nosed" might be represented as an ordered pair consisting of Socrates—the actual man, of course, not his name—and the predicate (or property, perhaps), being snub-nosed. (More complicated sentences, involving relations and more than one singular expression of this sort would be represented as ordered triplets, and so forth.) Now if someone were to say to Socrates, "You are snub-nosed," or Socrates were to say about himself, "I am snub-nosed," the proposition expressed would, in each case, be represented by the same ordered pair—propositional identity, given the same predicate, would be a function simply of what individual is referred to.

This way of representing propositions would, I think, meet with at least provisional approval by Russell, but only if it were restricted to those propositions expressed by statements containing "genuine" names. We might even say that the manner of representation gives a respectable sense in which an individual might be a constituent of a proposition. But my examples of statements for which this representation was suggested would, on Russell's view, be incorrect just because they involve singular terms from ordinary language. For Russell, they would be examples of sentences that express complex general propositions and, whatever our view of the nature of propositions, I do not think we would want propositional identity for general propositions to be a function of the individuals that happen to make the propositions true or false.

Russell pays the price, I believe, of giving up the natural view of many uses of ordinary singular terms, a price he is willing to pay—chiefly, perhaps, because he thus can dissolve puzzles about reference. The special properties of "genuine" names, on the other hand, are supposed to rescue them. The "natural" view, on the other hand, seems to generate Russell's budget of puzzles, in particular the one which is the concern of this paper. If I say, "Socrates is snub-nosed," the proposition I express is represented as containing Socrates. If I say, instead,

"Jacob Horn does not exist," the "natural" view seems to lead to the unwonted conclusion that even if what I say is true, Jacob Horn, though nonexistent, must have some reality. Else what proposition am I expressing? The "natural" view thus seems to land us with the Meinongian population explosion.

Russell, of course, avoids this problem easily. Since the proper name "Jacob Horn" would, for him, be a concealed definite description, to say "Jacob Horn does not exist" is not to refer to some individual in order to say something about him, but merely to assert that a particular class of things, perhaps the class of writers of diaries about certain events in early Pennsylvania history, is either empty or contains more than one member. (So a singular nonexistence statement of this kind is on all fours with statements such as "There are no flying horses" or "There is more than one living ex-President." It does not mention a particular individual any more than these do.)

The issue has importance for the historical explanation view because it denies that many singular terms in ordinary language, in particular proper names, are concealed descriptions of the sort that Russell had in mind. "Homer," for example, is not a concealed description such as "the author of the Homeric Poems," to use Russell's own example. The question is, does the historical explanation view, if correct, support what I have called the "natural" view? In the next section this question will be considered.

III. THE HISTORICAL EXPLANATION VIEW: NEGATIVE ASPECT

I now want to begin to lay out the bare bones of the theory of reference I want to discuss. As I have said, I will not here argue for its correctness nor will I try to fill in all the gaps.

Russell and the majority of philosophers in contemporary times who have discussed (ordinary) proper names have held that by one mechanism or another they are surrogates for descriptions. For Russell, as I have mentioned, they are simply abbreviations for definite descriptions; for others—for example, Searle[11]—they are correlated with a set of descriptions and what one is saying in, say, a simple subject-predicate sentence employing a proper name is that whatever best fits these descriptions has whatever property is designated by the predicate. The descriptions, both on Russell's view and on the looser view of Searle and others, which the proper name masks, are thought of as obtained from the people who use them—roughly speaking, by what they would answer to the question, "To whom (what) are you referring?" This view of ordinary proper names embodies what I have called the "principle of identifying descriptions."[12] The theory of reference I am concerned with holds that the principle of identifying descriptions is false.

What this means, to give an example, is that, supposing you could obtain from me a set of descriptions of who it is that I believe myself to refer to when I say, "Socrates was snub-nosed"—perhaps such things as "the mentor of Plato," "the inventor of the 'Socratic method,'" "the philosopher who drank the hemlock," and so forth—it is theoretically possible that I am referring to something about which no substantial number of these descriptions is true or that although there is something that fits these descriptions to whatever extent is required by the particular variation of the principle, that is not in fact the referent of the name I used.

On this theory, then, ordinary proper names are like Russell's "genuine" names at least insofar as they do not conceal descriptions in the way he thought. This is, I think, a virtue of the theory. As David Kaplan has remarked, there was always something implausible about the idea that a referent of a proper name is determined by the currently associated descriptions.

IV. THE HISTORICAL EXPLANATION THEORY: POSITIVE ASPECT

The first tenet of the theory of reference I have been describing was negative—the view that proper names must have a backing of descriptions that serves to pick out their referents is false. The second tenet is positive, but more tentative. How is the referent of a proper name, then, to be determined? On Russell's view and variants on it, the answer to this question would be simple: the referent is that which fits the associated descriptions best, where "best" may be defined differently by different writers. As I see it, one of the main reasons a backing of descriptions for proper names is so attractive is that it furnishes a simple way of ascertaining what a speaker is saying, and of determining whether what he says is true or false (given that we are dealing only with assertions). We find, so to speak, that thing in the world which uniquely fits the descriptions and then see whether or not it has the properties ascribed to it. If proper names do not have a backing of descriptions, how do we decide whether or not, when someone says, for example, "Russell wrote 'On Denoting,'" he has said something true or false?

Putting existence statements aside, when a speaker says something of the form, "$\mathcal{N}$ is ϕ," where "$\mathcal{N}$" is a name and "ϕ" a predicate, we can say that in general the truth conditions will have the following form. What the speaker has said will be true if and only if (*a*) there is some entity related in the appropriate way to his use of "$\mathcal{N}$" in this sentence—that is, he has referred to some entity, and (*b*) that entity has the property designated by ϕ. (I say "in general" because there are difficulties for any theory of reference about uses of names for fictional characters, "formal" objects such as numbers, and so forth.) The question is, what is the "appropriate relation" mentioned in condition (*a*)? How, that is, does an entity have to be related to the speaker's use of the name "$\mathcal{N}$" to be its referent? The principle of identifying descriptions, were it only true, has a simple answer to this: the entity must have (uniquely) the properties or some sufficient number of the properties designated by the "backing of descriptions" for this use of the name "$\mathcal{N}$." Roughly speaking, and on the most usual view, it will be the entity that answers to the descriptions the speaker would (ideally) give in answer to the question, "To whom are you referring?"

But even without the arguments that, I believe, show the principle of identifying descriptions not only false, but implausible, putting the matter in this general way is somewhat liberating. It shows that what we need is *some* relation between the speech act involving the name "$\mathcal{N}$" and an object in the world—the right one, of course—but the relation supplied by the principle of identifying descriptions is now only a candidate for that office.

But if the principle of identifying descriptions is false, what then is the appropriate relation between an act of using a name and some object such that the name was used to refer to that object? The theory of reference I want to discuss has not as yet, so far as I know, been developed in such a way as to give a completely detailed answer. Yet there are positive things that can be said and enough, I believe, both to contrast it with the principle of identifying descriptions and to give us something like an answer to the original question: how will it handle apparent reference to the nonexistent in such statements as "Santa Claus does not exist"?

The main idea is that when a speaker uses a name intending to refer to an individual and predicate something of it, successful reference will occur when there is an individual that enters into the historically correct explanation of who it is that the speaker intended to predicate something of. That individual will then be the referent and the statement made will be true or false depending upon whether it has the property designated by the predicate. This statement of the positive thesis leaves a lot to be desired in the way of precision, yet with some clarifying remarks I think it has more content than might at first sight be supposed.

Suppose someone says, "Socrates was snub-nosed," and we ask to whom he is referring. The central idea is that this calls for a historical explanation; we search not for an individual who might best fit the speaker's descriptions of the individual to whom he takes himself to be referring (though his descriptions are usually important data), but rather for an individual historically related to his use of the name "Socrates" on this occasion. It might be that an omniscient observer of history would see an individual related to an author of dialogues, that one of the central characters of these dialogues was modeled upon that individual, that these dialogues have been handed down and that the speaker has read translations of them, that the speaker's now predicating snub-nosedness of something is explained by his having read those translations. This is the sort of account that I have in mind by a "historical explanation."

Several comments are in order here. First, it is not necessary, of course, that the individual in question be snub-nosed; obviously the speaker may have asserted something false about the referent of the name "Socrates." Second, if we take the set of descriptions the speaker could give were we to ask him to whom he was referring, the historical explanation as seen by our omniscient observer may pick out an individual as the referent of the name "Socrates" even though that individual is not correctly described by the speaker's attempt at identification. For example, the speaker may believe that Socrates—

that is, the person he refers to—was a philosopher who invented the Socratic method. But it is clearly imaginable that our omniscient observer sees that while the author of the dialogues did intend one of the characters to be taken as a portrayal of a real person, he modestly attributed to him a method that was his own brain child. And, in general, it would be possible to have the historical connection with no end to mistaken descriptions in the head of the speaker. The descriptions the speaker gives, however, may play an important role, though not the one given to them by the principle of identifying descriptions. The omniscient observer may see, for example, that the reason the speaker believes himself to be referring to someone who invented a certain philosophical method is that his present use of the name "Socrates" is connected with his having read certain translations of these dialogues. Or, to take a slightly different case, he may see that his descriptions come from a faulty memory of those dialogues, and so forth. The question for the omniscient observer is "What individual, if any, would the speaker describe in this way even if perhaps mistakenly?"

I have used the notion of an omniscient observer of history and, of course, we ordinary people cannot be expected to know in detail the history behind the uses of names by those with whom we converse. Nor do we often make the sort of historical inquiries which would reveal those details. We often assume, for example, that if another speaker's descriptions of the referent of a name he has used more or less jibe with descriptions we would give of a person, place, or thing that we believe ourselves to know about, then he is referring to that. Also, for example, the context of the use of a name may lead us to assume without question that the speaker refers to someone with whom we are both acquainted. But the historical explanation theory need not deny this or be troubled by it. All it needs to hold is that the *final* test for reference is the kind of historical connection

I have described, that the customary assumptions and use of indicators are in the end dependent upon being fairly reliable guides to the existence of such a connection.

What the historical explanation theory must attempt to establish is that when there is an absence of historical connection between an individual and the use of a name by a speaker, then, be the speaker's descriptions ever so correct about a certain individual, that individual is not the referent; and, on the other hand, that a certain historical connection between the use of a name and an individual can make the individual the referent even though the speaker's descriptions would not by themselves single out the individual. This job must be accomplished by building up examples in which these two points are made obvious. We might, for instance, try to show that the historical connection is necessary by constructing a situation in which, for instance, one person begins by assuming that another is referring to a friend of his, perhaps because the descriptions seem accurate, the context is appropriate, and so forth, and who then discovers that it is practically impossible for the speaker to have been acquainted with or otherwise related to his friend. In such an event, surely confidence that the speaker was referring to the friend would be shaken despite the apparent accuracy of description or appropriateness of context. But, as I have said, I cannot here undertake the full defense of the historical explanation theory.

There are, however, two further points of clarification that ought to be mentioned here. It should be obvious that I have only provided an example of what counts as a historical explanation rather than a formula for obtaining the referent of a particular use of a name. Even in the illustration several individuals entered into the account, only one of which was the referent. Of the individuals who are in some way or other part of the historical explanation of a use of a name, which is the referent? What kind of theory is this if it does not give us the means to make this determination?

In defense against this charge that the theory is excessively vague, it is helpful, I think, to compare it with another philosophical theory about a quite different problem. The causal theory of perception can be taken as holding that an observer, *O*, perceives an object, *M*, only if *M* causes *O* to have sense impressions. The theory seems to me to have content and to be important, whether or not it is correct. For one thing, if true it means that certain other theories are mistaken. But the theory as stated does not, obviously, allow us to say which among the various causal factors involved in an observer having sense impressions is the thing he perceives; nor does it tell us which ways of causing sense impressions are relevant. Possibly no philosophical analysis can determine this, although in any particular case we may be able to say that this is or is not the right sort of causal connection. Analogously, the historical explanation theory lacks this sort of specificity. But for all that, if it is true, certain other theories, in particular the identifying descriptions theory, will be wrong and the theory does tell us something of importance.

Because there have sometimes been misunderstandings about this, I think I should point out that the history to which the historical explanation theory alludes is not the history of the use of a name. It is not the history of the use of, say, the name "Socrates" that is important. Socrates may not have been, as far as theory goes, called "Socrates"; corruption of names is just as possible as corruption of information. (The history of such a corruption, however, *might* enter into the historical explanation.) Nor, I think, should the theory be construed as holding that the historical connections end with some original "dubbing" of the referent. It may be that people, places, and things usually receive names by some such ceremony and that we generally use names (or corruptions of them) as a result of such a ceremony, but it is not a theoretical necessity that names enter our linguistic transactions in this way.[13]

What the historical explanation does, then, is to provide the relationship between the use of a referring expression and the referent which the principle of identifying descriptions presupposes could be provided only by some measure of correct descriptions of the referent known to the speaker. I think there are counter-examples to the principle of identifying descriptions[14] and, of course, if there *are* that defeats it straight off. Still a plausible, if not clearly correct, alternative theory in this case also acts as an objection. For one of the principle reasons that many philosophers have for adopting the principle of identifying descriptions is that they cannot see how there *could* be an appropriate relation otherwise that would pick out the referent of (as the main example) a proper name.

I have, in describing this theory of reference, talked about a "historical explanation." I hope it is obvious that "historical" is being used in the broadest sense possible; that all of what I have said could just as well be applied to cases in which one refers, by use of a name, say, to someone still extant, to someone who has just gone out of the room, or to someone presently in one's company. The "historical explanation," in other words, can involve as brief an interval of time as one pleases.

V. A SOLUTION TO THE PUZZLE REJECTED

My problem, then, is to show how such a theory of reference can deal with simple existence statements expressed by the use of a proper name, the difficulty being that on this theory, proper names do not have a backing of descriptions and, in general, they function to refer via what I have called a historical connection with some individual. But a true negative existence statement expressed by using a name involves a name with no referent and the corresponding positive existence statement, if false, will also. But in other contexts, when a name is used and there is a failure of reference, then no proposition has been expressed—certainly no true proposition. If a child says, "Santa Claus will come tonight," he cannot have spoken the truth, although, for various reasons, I think it better to say that he has not even expressed a proposition.[15]

One apparently possible solution to the problem must be rejected. Russell and others, as we have seen, thought of (ordinary) proper names as concealed definite descriptions; he held a version, that is, of the principle of identifying descriptions. Existential statements involving ordinary proper names were therefore no problem for him—they were really existential statements involving definite descriptions and could be analyzed in accordance with his theory of definite descriptions. The suggestion I want to look at is that while our theory tells us that names in predicative statements do not obey the principle of identifying descriptions and are not concealed definite descriptions, existential statements may represent a special case. Thus, so this suggestion would run, "Santa Claus" in "Santa Claus will come tonight" is not a concealed definite description, but *is* one in the special context of "Santa Claus does not exist" and "Santa Claus exists." This would, of course, immediately solve our problem, but unfortunately it is not a solution that our theory can accept. The difficulty is not that names would be treated as functioning differently in different contexts; in fact, as will become evident, my own view is that they do behave differently in existence statements. Rather, the trouble is that any theory that rejects the principle of identifying descriptions for predicative statements must also reject it for existence statements.

To simplify matters, let us restrict ourselves to Russell's version of the principle of identifying descriptions in which a name simply stands in place of some definite description. If we adopt the principle for existence statements involving names, this will come to saying that, for example, "Socrates did not exist" means the same thing as (expresses the same proposition as) some other sentence formed from this by replacing "Socrates" by a definite description—perhaps, say, the sentence, "The Greek philosopher who was convicted of corrupting the youth and drank hemlock did not exist." But, now, on any view we must, I think, accept the following:

> (*E*) That Socrates did not exist entails that it is not true that Socrates was snub-nosed.

Our theory tells us that the second occurrence of "Socrates" in (*E*) is not a concealed definite description. But then neither can the first occurrence be one. For if we take some definite description such as the one suggested as what the first occurrence of "Socrates" stands for, rejection of the principle of identifying descriptions for the second occurrence means that it *could* be true that Socrates was snub-nosed even though no unique individual existed who satisfied that description. That is to say, if "Socrates" in "Socrates did not exist" is a concealed definite description, but is not in "Socrates was snub-nosed," then the antecedent of (*E*) could be true while the consequent is false. Since we want to accept the entailment expressed by (*E*) our theory cannot treat "Socrates" as a concealed description in existential statements.

This solution not being open to us, we cannot on the other hand go to the opposite extreme and handle existential statements involving ordinary proper names in the way Russell did for what he called names "in the strict logical sense." There simply are no meaningful existential statements involving these "genuine" names and so the problem does not arise about how to deal with them. But, of course, we cannot countenance this about ordinary proper names, for it does make sense to say, "Homer existed" or "Santa Claus does not exist."

VI. TRUTH CONDITIONS AND "BLOCKS"

What we need to do first is see what, on our theory of reference, the truth conditions are going to look like for existence statements involving names. In predicative statements, such as "Homer was a great poet," if everything goes well, there will be some individual related to this use of "Homer" "historically," as I have put it, and the statement will be true if that individual had the property expressed by the predicate and false otherwise. This, of course, cannot be so for a negative existence statement such as "Homer did not exist." This statement would be true, in fact, just in case there is a failure of reference, not in the statement itself, but in other possible or actual predicative statements involving the name. That is, if there is no individual related historically in the right way to the use of "Homer" in, say, the statement "Homer was a great poet," no individual whose possession or nonpossession of poetic genius makes this true or false, then we can truly state that Homer did not exist.

Initially then the question comes to this: "What, on our theory, constitutes a failure of reference in a predicative statement involving a proper name?" (As we shall see there is more to the matter than just this.) Since the positive part of our theory, the part that attempts to say what successful reference to an individual consists in, has been, perhaps because of the nature of things, left more suggestive than in a rigorously formulated state, it cannot be hoped that we shall do much better with failure of reference. But we can say some things of a non-trivial nature.

Suppose a child who believed in Santa Claus now learns the truth, the truth which he expresses by saying, "Santa Claus does not exist." He comes to learn this, as usual, from cynical older children; what has he learned? Our account is that he has learned that when in the past he believed something, for example, which he would have expressed by saying, "Santa Claus comes tonight," and would have thought himself in saying this to be referring to someone, the historical explanation of this belief does not involve any individual who could count as the referent of "Santa Claus"; rather it ends in a story given to him by his parents, a story told to him as factual. I do not mean, of course, that the child would or could express the knowledge he has in his new state of disillusionment in this fashion—that would require him to know the correct account of reference. But if *we* are approaching the correct theory, then this is how we can state what he has discovered.

When the historical explanation of the use of a name (with the intention to refer) ends in this way with events that preclude any referent being identified, I will call it a "block" in the history. In this example, the block is the introduction of the name into the child's speech via a fiction told to him as reality by his parents. Blocks occur in other ways. For example, children often invent imaginary companions whom they themselves come to speak of as actual. The block in such a case would occur at the point at which a name for the unreal companion gets introduced by the child himself via his mistaken belief that there is a companion to name. A somewhat different example would be this: suppose the Homeric poems were not written by one person, but were a patchwork of the writings of many people, combined, perhaps, with fragments from an oral tradition. Suppose, further, that at some point in time an ancient scholar for whatever reasons—he might have seen a name attached to some written version of the poems and supposed it to be the name of the author—attributed the poems to a single person he called "Homer." If this were the historical explanation of our saying, for example, "Homer wrote the *Iliad*," then the block occurs at the point at which this scholar enters the picture.

On theories that subscribe to the principle of identifying descriptions, examples of failure of reference such as occur in this last example would be treated as a failure to satisfy a uniqueness condition. The reason that Homer would not have existed given these circumstances is that no single individual satisfies the descriptions we associate with Homer (or satisfies a "sufficient" number, according to certain views). But according to our theory this is not the reason for failure of reference; it is rather that the history of our use of the name, a history with which we may not be familiar, does not end in the right way. One way to see that the opposing account, though plausible, is wrong is to think of the possibility of someone existing who *does* satisfy the descriptions we might supply of the referent of a name we use, but who has no historical connection with us whatsoever. Suppose, for example, that contrary to what we adults believe we know, there is, in fact, a man with a long white beard and a belly like a bowl full of jelly who comes down chimneys on Christmas night to leave gifts (the ones whose labels are missing about which parents worry because they don't know to what aunt the child should write a thank-you note). We must, of course, imagine that it is absolutely fortuitous that our descriptions of Santa Claus happen to fit so accurately this jolly creature. In that case I do not think that he *is* Santa Claus. The fact that the story of Santa Claus, told to children as fact, is historically an invention constitutes a block even if the story happens to contain only descriptions that accurately fit some person.

VII. A RULE FOR NEGATIVE EXISTENCE STATEMENTS

Using the technical, but admittedly not well-defined, notion of a "block," we can now sketch the way the historical explanation theory may treat negative existence statements involving names. A similar treatment could then be given for positive existence statements.

I will suggest a rule, using the notion of a block, that purports to give the truth conditions for negative existence statements containing a name. This rule, however, does not provide an *analysis* of such statements; it does not tell us what such statements mean or what proposition they express. This means that in this case we are divorcing truth conditions from meaning.

With the deletion of some qualifications that would be needed to make it strictly correct, the rule can be expressed as follows:

> (*R*) If $\mathcal{N}$ is a proper name that has been used in predicative statements with the intention to refer to some individual, then ⌈$\mathcal{N}$ does not exist⌉ is true if and only if the history of those uses ends in a block.

The rule as stated obviously requires some modifications. For one thing we would need some way of distinguishing, for example, the denial of the existence of Aristotle the philosopher, from Aristotle the ship magnate. To accomplish this we must do two things: first, find a means of collecting together the uses of "Aristotle" in predicative statements that were, so to speak, attempts to refer to the philosopher, separating them from a similar collection of uses of the name that were attempts to refer to the ship magnate, and do this without, of course, assuming that any of these uses succeeds in referring. Second, we must be able to relate a particular negative existence statement using the name "Aristotle" to one such collection rather than any other.

The way of amending Rule (*R*) that seems to me in keeping with the historical explanation theory and to accomplish these tasks is this. Certain uses of the name "Aristotle" in predicative statements will have similar histories, histories that will distinguish them from other uses of the name. Each use of the name will, of course, have its own historical explanation, but these may, at a certain point, join up. So, in tracing back several uses of the name "Aristotle" by me and several uses by you, we may find a common root in certain ancient writings and documents, while other uses of the name by me or by you may have nothing in common with the history of the first set of uses. It is possible that the histories may join at what I have called a block. Another possibility, however, is that although different uses of the name end in different blocks, these blocks are themselves historically connected. This might occur, for example, for the use by different children of the name "Santa Claus." I have suggested that the block in this example occurs where the parents tell the children a fiction as if it were fact. The block, however, would be a different one for each child. Still the blocks themselves are historically related in an obvious way since the parents' deception is rooted in a common tradition.

Still another possible source of difficulty with Rule (*R*) as stated is that it makes use of prior instances of the name in predicative statements. Is it possible meaningfully to assert "$\mathcal{N}$ does not exist" when $\mathcal{N}$ has never been used in predicative statements (about actuality)? If it is, then Rule (*R*) would have to be amended in some way, perhaps by talking of potential or possible uses. But at the moment I am not sure how this would go and I will not attempt it.

Even without worrying about the vagueness of the idea of a "block," Rule (*R*) may look unexciting, but its consequences are interesting. In the first place its form is completely antithetical to the principle of identifying descriptions, for it has nothing to do with whether an individual of a certain description existed or not. Second, it does not involve our theory of reference in any difficulties: there is the connection with the notion of historical explanation and so it ties in neatly with the positive aspects of the view, but it has no Meinongian implications, no overpopulation with entities whose existence is being denied. This result is bought, to be sure, at the price of making a name function differently in existence statements as opposed to predicative statements. But, as I have said, I think that this is not an unintuitive result.

While the above are important consequences of (*R*), what interests me about (*R*) is that it gives the truth conditions for statements that assert that some *individual* does not exist in terms of a linguistic failure—the failure of a name to refer on account of a "block." And it should occur to one that there may be something wrong with this. How, it might be asked, can Homer's existence or nonexistence be a matter of a fact about language, a fact about the name "Homer"? One is reminded, at this point, of a similar problem connected with the other puzzle about reference mentioned at the beginning of this paper. In "On Sense and Reference," immediately after propounding the puzzle about identity statements, Frege mentions a solution that he had formerly thought correct, but which he now repudiates just because it seems to involve turning identity statements, which apparently express facts about the world, into statements about a particular language.

Rule (*R*), insofar as it is supposed to express truth conditions for negative existence statements of a certain kind, seems objectionable for the same reasons. The crux of the problem in both cases seems to be this. We are inclined to say that the propositions expressed by us as "The Evening Star is identical with the Morning Star" and "Homer did not exist" can be the very same propositions that someone else may express using entirely different names. Therefore, how can we give a rule, such as (*R*), which makes the truth conditions of what we say depend upon facts about particular names?

The child who has become disillusioned expresses his new-found knowledge by saying "Santa Claus doesn't exist." A French-speaking child, with a similar history of being deceived by adults, might express his discovery by saying, "*Père Noël n'existe pas.*" Although the names are different, I believe we should want to say that the two children have learned the same fact and, on that account, that they have expressed the same proposition. Yet if we apply Rule (*R*) to each case it seems that the truth conditions must be different; they involve a block in the history of the use of the name "Santa Claus" for the English-speaking child and a block for the French-speaking child in the history of the use of the different name, "Père Noël."

Perhaps we can see the problem more clearly by looking for a moment at predicative statements. If we consider a simple (grammatically) subject-predicate statement, such as "Socrates is bald," and think of this as divided into its referring element, "Socrates," and its predicative element, "is bald," then if a certain change in the predicative element—for example, from "is bald" to "is short"—results in a change in the truth conditions for the statement, we want to say that the result expresses a different proposition. In general only interchange of synonymous predicates will maintain the same truth conditions and the same proposition. *If* referring expressions such as "Socrates" *were* concealed descriptions—that is, introduced predicate elements into a statement—then the same could be said about them: substituting a different referring expression, unless it happened to conceal the same or synonymous descriptions as the one it is substituted for, would shift both the truth conditions and the proposition expressed (and, in fact, this is the heart of Frege's way of avoiding his puzzle about identity statements).

But our theory of reference denies that referring expressions such as "Socrates" conceal descriptions or introduce predicate elements. If we keep the predicative element the same and substitute a different referring expression—say, "Plato" for "Socrates"—then whether or not we have the same proposition expressed depends solely upon whether or not the same thing is referred to. And this in turn depends upon whether the historical explanation of the use of these two expressions traces back to the same individual. If you say "Henry is bald" and I say "George is bald" we express the same proposition if the person you referred to by using the name "Henry" and I by using the name "George" are the same person. But what you say is true if and only if the person you referred to—that is, the person historically connected—when you used the name "Henry" has the property of being bald; whereas what I say is true if and only if what I referred to by using the name "George" has the property of being bald. The truth conditions are different because they must be stated in terms of what is referred to by different expressions, in the one case my use of the name "George" and in the other your use of the name "Henry." Yet we may express the same proposition.

So with predicative statements involving proper names, given the same predicate, sameness or difference of propositions comes down to sameness or difference of the referent of the names. It seems that if we try to state the truth conditions for a particular use of such a statement, we are not going to arrive at what we should like to call the proposition expressed. But although we thus are separating truth conditions from propositions expressed, the latter notion is still a fairly clear concept. It seems, however, that we cannot in the same way preserve a clear notion of what proposition is expressed for existence statements involving proper names.

Our problem arose because we wanted on the one hand to make it possible that one child saying "Santa Claus does not exist" may express the same proposition as another who says "*Père Noël n'existe pas.*" But, on the other hand, our explanation of the truth conditions for such statements in Rule (*R*) made them different for the two cases. We have seen, however, that if the historical explanation theory is correct, a difference in truth conditions without a shift in proposition expressed can occur in any case with predicative statements. This can occur when there is a difference in names used without a change in referent. So this seems to be a general feature of the theory's treatment of names. When we turn to negative existence statements and Rule (*R*), however, we cannot give as a criterion for propositional identity sameness of referent. For, of course, if true, the name in such a statement has no referent.

What we would like, still continuing with the example, is a reason for saying that both children express the same proposition that is at once in line with our theory and intuitively satisfying. I want to suggest that we may find such a reason once more by using the idea of a historical connection, that, in our example, it is the blocks in the historical explanation of the use respectively of the names "Santa Claus" and "Père Noël" that are themselves historically connected. Once again, I do not have the resources to spell out a general principle for what this historical connection must be, any more than I did with the notion of a block itself. Yet in the example before us, and others one can think of, our inclination to say that people using different names express the same negative existence proposition seems to be a matter of historical connection between the blocks involved. In our example, it seems to me that the reason we think both children express the same proposition is that the story of Santa Claus and the story of Père Noël, the stories passed on to the two children as if they were factual, have a common root. And if there were not this common history, I think we should rather hold that the two children believed similar, perhaps, but not identical falsehoods, for example, when the one attributed gifts to Santa Claus and the other to Père Noël and that they expressed different truths when one said "Santa Claus does not exist" and the other said "*Père Noël n'existe pas.*"

VIII. CONCLUDING REMARKS

If this discussion has been on the right track, then at least the outline of a solution to some problems concerning nonexistence statements is available to the historical explanation theory. One point emerged in the course of the last sections. We can perhaps point to criteria for saying when two existence statements involving names express the same proposition, but these criteria take a different form from those for predicative statements involving names. In particular, it cannot be a matter of sameness of referent. For predicative statements we were able to suggest a way of representing propositions, as ordered *n*-tuplets, but no obvious way of representing propositions expressed by existence statements suggests itself. This does not seem to me to count against the theory, since the notion of a proposition is not, I think, a clear one that has established use outside of a theory. The fact that the representation suggested for predicative statements involving proper names has no counterpart for existence statements, however, may account in part for the fact that Russell took the alternatives for proper names to be either a Meinongian view or a concealed descriptions view. For the representation of propositions suggested is, I think, essentially Russellian and either of these views of ordinary proper names would allow him to apply it to existence statements.

NOTES

1. Earlier versions of this paper were read at a number of meetings and colloquia and several important changes have resulted from those discussions. I am particularly grateful for detailed comments by Tyler Burge.
2. Reprinted in *Logic and Knowledge*, ed. by Marsh (1956), p. 47.
3. Why I am reluctant to use the word "causal" may become somewhat clearer further on, but the main reason is that I want to avoid a seeming commitment to all the links in the referential chain being causal.
4. *Translations from the Philosophical Writings of Gottlob Frege*, ed. by Geach and Black (1952).
5. Reprinted in *Logic and Knowledge*.
6. If we divide the theory into its negative aspects (see sec. III) and its positive (see sec. IV), what the theory denies and the reasons for doing so have been, perhaps, better delineated in the literature than the content of the positive theory. (This is certainly true of my own contributions.) My papers dealing with various parts of the theory as I see it are: "Reference and Definite Descriptions," *Philosophical Review*, LXXV (1966), 281–304; "Putting Humpty Dumpty Together Again," *Philosophical Review*, LXXVII (1968), 203–15; "Proper Names and Identifying Descriptions," *Synthèse* (1970), reprinted in Davidson and Harman (eds.), *Semantics of Natural Language* (Dordrecht, 1972). By others, Saul Kripke's paper, "Naming and Necessity," in *Semantics of Natural Language*, is the most important in that it gives not only arguments for the negative aspects of the theory, but also a positive account (that, however, I do not altogether agree with).
7. The terminology, of course, is for convenience and not supposed to reflect a prejudgment that existence cannot be in some sense a genuine predicate.
8. See Middleton and Adair, "The Mystery of the Horn Papers," *William and Mary Quarterly*, 3rd series, IV (1947); reprinted in Winks (ed.), *The Historian as Detective* (New York, 1968).
9. The denial of Snow White's existence, it should be noted, is in discourse about actuality, while the statement that she enraptured a prince is in discourse about fiction. (If the question of existence arose in discourse about fiction alone, Snow White existed, whereas Hamlet's father's ghost, again presuming we are talking about fiction, probably did not.) This does not disturb the point: no such contrast can be made out for Jacob Horn; if Jacob Horn did not exist then there are no true predicative statements to be made about him.
10. E.g., J. Searle, "Proper Names," *Mind* (1958), and *Speech Acts* (Cambridge, 1968), Ch. IV.
11. See references in n. 10.
12. In "Proper Names and Identifying Descriptions," *op. cit.*
13. That is to say, the first use of a name to refer to some particular individual might be in an assertion about him, rather than any ceremony of *giving* the individual that name. (In fact, my own name is an example: I discovered that colleagues

were pronouncing my last name differently than my parents do—so, orally, they referred to me by a different name—and I let it stand. But I was never dubbed by that new name. I am sure that the first use of it was either an assertion, question, or whatever about me and not a kind of baptism. And I think it is probable that whatever audience there was knew to whom the speaker referred.)

14. See my "Proper Names and Identifying Descriptions," *op. cit.*
15. Given that this is a statement about reality and that proper names have no descriptive content, then how are we to represent the proposition expressed?

[5]

SPEAKER REFERENCE, DESCRIPTIONS, AND ANAPHORA

People refer and expressions refer. Let us call these phenomena "speaker reference" and "semantic reference" respectively.[1] What connection exists between the two? The question has importance for how we theorize about various referring expressions, demonstratives, for example. And it is fairly crucial for what significance should be attached to a distinction I proposed some time back between what I called two uses of definite descriptions, the referential and the attributive.[2] At the time I thought of the distinction as having importance beyond a contribution to the understanding of how definite descriptions work and the problems it seemed to pose for the theories of Russell and Strawson on that matter, precisely because it apparently showed the necessity of bringing in speaker reference for an explanation of the semantic reference of certain expressions.

While the referential/attributive distinction proves, I believe, to appeal to our intuitions, vagueness about the role of speaker reference threatens its significance. Are there two *uses* of definite descriptions in the sense of two semantic functions in one of which the description

First published in *Syntax and Semantics*, Vol. 9. *Pragmatics*. P. Cole, ed., New York: Academic Press, 1978, pp. 47–68.

conveys speaker reference and in the other not? Or is it rather that definite descriptions are used in two kinds of circumstances, in one of which there is an accompanying phenomenon of speaker reference though it has no effect on the semantic reference of the description? If the latter, it is not clear what importance we should attach to the distinction in the philosophy of language. It would not, for example, seem to have a bearing on the correctness or incorrectness of a semantic analysis of sentences containing definite descriptions such as Russell gives us.

I want to investigate this matter further in this paper and I offer certain arguments derived from a consideration of the phenomenon of anaphora to show that speaker reference cannot be divorced from semantic reference.

I

It would no doubt be enlightening were I to begin by saying what speaker reference consists in. We naturally gravitate to such expressions as "what the speaker had in mind" that echo locutions from ordinary speech—"Whom do you have in mind?" But what is it to have someone or something in mind? Is it, for example, to possess a body of descriptions that identify a particular person or thing? I will not attempt, however, any general answer to this important problem. Instead, I will rely on what I think is the indisputable fact that there is something corresponding to these locutions and go on to ask where it fits into the theory of reference. I believe, in fact, that even those who find little use for a notion of speaker reference acknowledge that the phenomenon occurs. Here, for example, is what Peter Geach says about it in *Reference and Generality*:

> Personal reference—i.e. reference corresponding to the verb "refer" as predicated of persons rather than of expressions

> [I take it this is what I am calling "speaker reference"]—is of negligible importance for logic; and I mention it only to get it out of the way. Let me take an example: Smith says indignantly to his wife, "The fat old humbug we saw yesterday has just been made a full professor!" His wife may know whom he refers to, and will consider herself misinformed if and only if that person has not been made a full professor. But the actual expression "the fat old humbug we saw yesterday" will refer to somebody only if Mr. and Mrs. Smith did meet someone rightly describable as a fat old humbug on the day before Smith's indignant remark; if this is not so, then Smith's actual words will not have conveyed true information, even if what Mrs. Smith gathered from them was true.[3]

Whatever we finally decide about the nature of the distinction, I believe we have enough raw intuitions about it often to be able to tell, given a sufficiently rich description of the circumstances, whether a particular example falls on the referential or the attributive side. Geach's description of this speech act pretty clearly makes it an example falling on the referential side.

Geach tells us that speaker reference is of "negligible importance for logic." I think we can fairly substitute for "logic," "semantics." In any event the specific conclusion we are to draw from the illustration is clear: the speaker's reference in no way determines the semantic reference of the expression he used. The two referents may, of course, be identical, but they may also diverge. The person Mr. Smith has in mind, the one he wants to inform his wife has been made full professor, may not in fact fit the description Smith used, may not be a fat old humbug whom they met the day before. In that event, while Mr. Smith can be said to have referred to whoever it was he had in mind, the uttered description did not. If it referred at all, it would be someone who did (uniquely I suppose) fit the description—even someone whom Mr. Smith has forgotten entirely and who never enters the heads of him or his wife during their conversation. Moreover, as Geach makes clear in the passage following the one quoted, the truth or falsity of what was *said* by Smith, as opposed to what he may have wanted to convey to his wife, depends in that event not on the properties of the person Mr. Smith has in mind to inform his wife about but upon the properties of that person who fits the uttered description. In this way Smith's words have, so to speak, a semantic life of their own. I believe that Geach intends the divorce of speaker and semantic reference to be a quite general across-the-board matter. And I think he is not alone among philosophers in supposing this to be so.[4]

In Geach's example we may suppose that Mr. Smith believes that a certain person he and his wife met the day before is a fat old humbug; he believes, that is, that a particular person he has in mind satisfies the description uttered. Perhaps we should add that this is likely an active belief—one that he has currently before his mind. Could this be all that speaker reference in such a case amounts to? If it is, then the referential/attributive distinction would presumably come to no more than this, that sometimes a speaker uses a definite description with an accompanying (active) belief about somebody or something that it fits the description and sometimes with no such accompaniment. Construed thusly, the distinction would be real enough, but, to be sure, of no interest for semantics and of little interest, one would think, even for a total theory of speech acts. A myriad of things accompany every speech act—beliefs, desires, itches, and, of course, various external circumstances. A division of speech acts or of a particular kind of speech act based merely on cooccurrence or lack of it between the speech act and some other event promises little for the theory of language. Even some connection between the accompanying item and, say, the content of the utterance will not by itself warrant much attention. Some utterances of the form "All X's are Y's," for instance, are undoubtedly accompanied by an active belief of the speaker's to the effect that the world contains too many X's and others are not. The distinction is real enough, but unlikely to find a place in any treatise on the philosophy of language.

II

The account of speaker reference just given, however, is obviously too thin. In the first place, it ignores the speaker's intentions toward his audience with respect to what he has in mind. In Geach's example, Mr. Smith intends his wife to recall some particular person met by them the day before and through that, together with his statement, to become informed of a fact about that person. Moreover, it is surely by his having produced the description "the fat old humbug we met yesterday" together, perhaps, with the circumstances of the utterance, that he intends she shall recollect that person. Such intentions can be crucial for the existence of speaker reference. Suppose in some appropriate setting I say, "The strongest man in the world can lift at least 450 lbs." I might have as my grounds for stating this some general considerations about the limits of human strength with no belief about anyone in particular that he is the strongest man in the world. In such an event there is, of course, nothing we can identify as speaker reference. But my grounds might still be those general considerations while I happen, in fact, to believe about some particular person, Vladimir Jones, say, that he is the strongest man. The addition of this belief should not make us talk of speaker reference. Suppose, though, that my grounds for my statement are that I believe of Vladimir that he is the strongest and I believe *he* can lift 450 lbs. Still, those are my *grounds* and if I do not expect nor intend that my audience shall recognize that I want to talk about Vladimir and to become informed about *his* strength, we have no reason to say that referred to Vladimir. What I have been describing, of course, is a case of what I would call an attributive use of a definite description. And what I am saying comes to this, that the referential/attributive distinction and the presence or absence of speaker reference should be thought of as based on such speaker intentions toward his audience or the lack of them—not on whether the speaker believes or not about someone or something that he or it fits the description.[5] (Later I will give a more fundamental criterion for speaker reference that will require modifications in what is said here about speaker intentions for a certain range of cases, but for the sort of example Geach gives us it will still be correct.)

The focus of interest of both speaker and audience in the sort of situation Geach describes surely lies in the speaker's reference. And we have in language various resources for asking questions about what the speaker refers to. The speaker's audience will not infrequently fail to recognize what he has in mind to talk about just from the uttered description and the context. It then becomes appropriate to ask him for more information. This may take the form of a simple request—"Whom do you mean?" "What are you talking about?"; or a request that the speaker provide further particulars in order to distinguish among several things that seem to fit the description he used—"Which fat old humbug? We met a couple of them yesterday"; or a question asking whether the speaker's referent fits also some further description—"Do you mean the boring old geezer with the goatee?" It also is not unnatural, we might note, to speak as if the speaker's reference were connected to the expression uttered, for example, "Whom do you mean by 'the fat old humbug we met yesterday'?"

The very form of these questions makes it hard to deny that they concern speaker reference. And in fact they are only appropriate when the speaker did intend to convey a reference. In the example given above in which when uttering "The strongest man in the world can lift 450 lbs.," the speaker had no intention of having his audience recognize him as referring to anyone in particular, it would have been out of place for his audience to ask him, for example, "Whom do you mean?" or "Are you talking about the Russian who won the gold medal?" or "By 'the strongest man in the world' are you referring to Vladimir Jones?" To do so would be to misread the situation and the speaker in turn may correct the misimpression by saying, for example, "I don't mean anyone in particular, just whoever is the strongest." Now if these questions were not about the speaker's reference but about the denotation of the description (whatever satisfied it uniquely), then there would be no reason why they should be appropriate only in the presence of speaker reference.

III

If the audience questions discussed in the last section are questions about the speaker's reference, as they certainly seem to be, I believe we can also show that in the circumstances in which they are appropriate, audience responses can also contain expressions whose referents are determined by what the original speaker had in mind; that here, at least, we have semantic reference determined by speaker reference. And that, I believe, was what Geach wished to deny took place when he said that we could conveniently ignore speaker reference when pursuing logic or, as I would rather say, semantics. But before showing this I want to introduce a notion I will have occasion to use in what follows.

In recent work Charles Chastain[6] has pointed to the importance for the theory of reference of what he calls "anaphoric chains." By these he means sequences of singular terms that are such that if one of them refers to something, they all do. A pronoun with an antecedent in the same sentence provides the simplest example:

(1) Mary is coming to town and John will meet her.

The pronoun "her" is coreferential with the name "Mary," and the two form what Chastain calls an anaphoric chain. There can be more than one chain in a single sentence, of course:

(2) John went to meet Tom and he waited for him almost two hours.

Here "he" is linked with "John" and "him" with "Tom." If we ask how we know which pronouns belong to which chains, I imagine that at least in some instances it has to do with rules of syntax discoverable by linguists—perhaps something to do with order of occurrence or possibly with a linking of subject to subject and object to object.

The phenomenon I want to exploit is not confined to the limits of single sentences. Chains can pass over sentence boundaries:

(3) John went to meet Tom. Does anyone know whether he has brought him back yet?

Here the pronouns of the second sentence take as antecedents names in the first. Or, to be more precise, they would do so on a natural interpretation and within the same stretch of discourse. If the sentences are uttered on widely separated occasions, for example, or if the utterance of the second sentence is accompanied by demonstrations giving the pronouns independent reference, then no such linkage will probably exist.

More important, chains can pass over speaker boundaries. In (3) the second sentence could have been uttered by someone other than the person who uttered the first. If that person is among the first speaker's audience, then the pronouns of the second sentence may be parasitic on the names used by the first speaker forming anaphoric chains with them. We will make use of this fact in what follows.

In general, there will be one member of an anaphoric chain that determines the referent of each of the other members and without which the other members would be left dangling. In the examples so far given proper names have served this function and pronouns have been parasitic on them. I will assume, for simplicity, that this determining member of the chain occurs first and call it the antecedent.[7]

IV

Let us say that a definite description is uttered in a "referential context" when speaker reference exists relative to it. So far, all this will mean is that the speaker intends to refer to something and intends his audience to recognize his reference in part through his having used that definite description. Thus in introducing this terminology we are not begging the issue, for example, as against Geach. Similarly, a definite description will be uttered in an attributive context when speaker reference relative to it is absent. Definite descriptions in attributive contexts can serve as the antecedent in an anaphoric chain. Imagine the following to be uttered in an attributive context relative to the definite description that forms the subject of the first sentence:

(4) The strongest man in the world can lift at least 450 lbs. He can also win a tug-of-war with a jackass.

In a suitable context the pronoun "he" in the second sentence forms an anaphoric chain with the definite description in the first; they both refer to the same thing if they refer at all. And what they both would refer to is undoubtedly the denotation of the definite description—that person, in this example, who uniquely fits the description. The pronoun, in fact, can be regarded as what Geach called a pronoun of laziness[8]—simply a means of avoiding repetition of the description. Now let us return to Geach's example, which, we are assuming, contains a definite description in a referential context, and extend the dialogue a bit.

(5) [Mr. Smith] The fat old humbug we met yesterday has just been made a full professor. He must have bamboozled the committee.

We seem once more to have an anaphoric chain. Certainly there is some link between the pronoun in the second sentence and the definite description in the first. And one would suppose they are coreferential, if they refer at all. If so, what do they both refer to? On the view that speaker reference and semantic reference are to be kept in their separate realms, the answer is clear: they both refer to the denotation of the description, if it has one. What this means is that if the person Mr. Smith has in mind, *his* reference, does not in fact fit the description, "the fat old humbug we met yesterday," what his second sentence expresses will be true just in case there was a (unique) fat old humbug he and his wife met the day before and who bamboozled the committee. And this would be so even if that person never enters into the Smiths' heads. If semantic reference is to be kept untainted by speaker reference, the pronouns in such anaphoric chains must be kept pure also.

But now recall that an audience may ask questions about the speaker's reference when it exists. So the conversation between the Smiths might have proceeded in this way:

(6) [Mr. Smith] The fat old humbug we met yesterday has just been made a full professor.
[Mrs. Smith] Do you mean the funny little man with the goatee?

But her query, which we have argued concerns Mr. Smith's reference, could have been cast into a sentence employing a pronoun:

(7) [Mrs. Smith] Is he the funny little man with the goatee?

If this is just another way of posing the same question, as I think it is, it too is a question about the speaker's reference. But then the pronoun "he" must refer to the referent of the speaker—to whatever person Mr. Smith was referring to.

An even more striking way of getting this result comes from considering the fact that an audience will sometimes disagree about the applicability of the description the speaker used. And such disagreement can hardly be a question of whether the description applies to its own denotation. Thus in the Smiths' conversation, Mrs. Smith might have said at a certain point:

(8) [Mrs. Smith] I don't think he's fat; he's just large boned. And as for his being a humbug, he seemed quite genuine and above board.

It would make nonsense of Mrs. Smith's comments to suppose that the third-person pronouns they contain are "pronouns of laziness" standing in for Mr. Smith's original description or that their referent is to be the denotation, if it has one, of that description. Surely it is Mr. Smith's reference that is in question and which determines the referent of these pronouns.

The Smiths' dialogue might have gone like this:

> [MR. SMITH] The fat old humbug we met yesterday has just been made a full professor. He must have bamboozled the committee.
>
> [MRS. SMITH] Is he the one with the funny goatee?
>
> [MR. SMITH] He's the one I mean.
>
> [MRS. SMITH] I don't think we met him yesterday. Wasn't it Friday?
>
> [MR. SMITH] I think you're right. He was coming from a faculty meeting, so it must have been a weekday.

We have an initial definite description followed by a string of pronouns in subsequent utterances. Some of those surely must take as their referent the man Mr. Smith has in mind, the speaker reference rather than whoever is denoted by the description, supposing it does have a denotation.

Now the (third-person) pronouns in this discourse fragment *seem* to form an anaphoric chain and the initial definite description *seems* to be the antecedent. If this were so, it would follow that the speaker's reference determines the semantic reference throughout.

I suppose that it would be possible to maintain that despite these data the truth or falsity of the utterance containing the definite description depends upon the properties of the denotation of the description, if it has one, and that *its* semantic referent is its denotation—even if this is not so for subsequent pronouns that seem on the surface to be anaphorically linked with it. There would certainly be complications for such a view. In the conversation as recorded Mr. Smith said "He must have bamboozled the committee" immediately following his utterance containing the definite description. Is this occurrence of the pronoun "he" anaphorically linked with the definite description? If so, would it no longer be had he produced this utterance *after* the Smiths had agreed that the original description was inapplicable?

In any event, some ground will have to be ceded. It will not be possible to set aside speaker reference as of no importance in the determination of semantic reference. For if speaker reference does not determine semantic reference in certain instances of the use of definite descriptions, it does for subsequent pronouns in some stretches of discourse containing them. The referential/attributive distinction, rested on the notion of speaker reference, will have semantic importance because it will mark the dichotomy between occurrences of definite descriptions that can initiate strings of pronouns whose reference depends upon the speaker's reference and those that do not.

V

I now want to turn to some further facts about definite descriptions and anaphoric chains that bear on the topic of speaker reference. Philosophers have often contrasted definite and indefinite descriptions. Definite descriptions, it is said, are used to speak of some one particular thing while indefinite descriptions are not. In the recent essay already mentioned Charles Chastain[9] has challenged this as a universal rule. Without for the moment assessing this interesting conclusion of his, I want to examine some of the facts that he uses in arriving at it.

It is certainly true that sometimes a use of an indefinite description in no way involves a reference to a particular thing while a shift to the definite article in the same context *would* indicate such a reference. We can correctly answer the question "Have you ever seen an elephant?" by saying, "Yes, I have seen an elephant" even if one has in fact seen many elephants. And in so answering, no one of the elephants seen has been singled out. But a particular elephant is presumably referred to if the question is "Have you seen the elephant?" and the answer is "Yes, I have seen the elephant."

The definite article indicates in some sense that a particular reference is being made,[10] but how does that get accomplished? We know that according to Russell's theory sentences containing definite descriptions (where they are what he called "primary" occurrences) assert in part that one thing uniquely has the properties ascribed by the description. Thus, provided that this part of what is asserted is true, some one particular thing gets singled out. This contrasts with the Russellian treatment of indefinite descriptions according to which sentences containing these expressions assert the existence of members in a certain class but do not, relative to the occurrences of indefinite descriptions, assert that there is a unique member.

There are two well-known difficulties with this treatment of definite descriptions as far as ordinary speech goes. One is that the definite article can accept plural noun phrases—"I have seen the elephants." The second is that definite descriptions perhaps most frequently found in ordinary discourse are too "indefinite" to allow us to suppose that their users intend to assert that some particular thing alone has the properties they ascribe. There are a large number of elephants in the world even today and most people who might have occasion to use the sentence "I have seen the elephant" are surely aware of this.

It is not clear how an account along strictly Russellian lines would get over the first of these difficulties, but a view suggested by Zeno Vendler[11] might provide a beginning. He says of the assertion "I know the men who fought in Korea" that it would imply that "... in some sense or other, I know all those men." And "It transpires, then, that the definite article marks the speaker's intention to exhaust the range determined by [the description]."[12] Singular definite descriptions would be a limiting case where it is asserted or implied that the range is limited to a single item. (Later I will try to show that this account fails.)

The second difficulty remains even on Vendler's view. That the descriptive content of many of the definite descriptions we actually utter is too meager to suppose that we mean to imply that they fit something uniquely has frequently not been taken seriously enough. The usual attempt at saving the situation is well known. The idea is that in ordinary speech we rely on attendant circumstances to supply implicit qualifications on the description actually uttered. So, "I have seen the elephant" uttered at the San Diego Zoo, with speaker and audience aware of their location, succeeds in being an utterance about a particular elephant because the speaker presumes that his audience will take his description as qualified by the restriction "at the San Diego Zoo" or some other qualification such as "at this zoo" that does the same work. This is not without plausibility for a large number of cases, but I believe it will not work as a general rule. Interestingly enough, nowhere do we find more intransigent examples than among the sorts of uses of definite descriptions investigated by Vendler that led him to the view of the definite article just mentioned.

Definite descriptions not only serve as antecedents in anaphoric chains, they also can act as later links in such a chain. Chastain's essay points to the importance of such occurrences of definite descriptions for the theory of reference. Now, interestingly, given the great contrast that is supposed to exist between definite and indefinite descriptions, the antecedents of such anaphoric chains turn out to be sentences containing indefinite descriptions. Consider the following discourse fragment:

(9) A man carne to the office today. He tried to sell me an encyclopedia.

The pronoun beginning the second sentence seems clearly to be connected in some fashion to the first sentence, though whether anaphorically linked in particular to the indefinite description "a man" is another question.[13] The pronoun can be replaced without any shift in what we would understand as being said by a definite description. In fact, as both Chastain and Vendler point out, a definite rather than an indefinite description is required to preserve the anaphoric linkage. We cannot read the following discourse fragment as saying that the same man who carne to the office tried to sell the speaker an encyclopedia; in fact, it is most naturally read as implying that there were two distinct men:

(10) A man carne to the office today. A man tried to sell me an encyclopedia.

The required definite description can be formed from the preceding sentence in one of two ways, either from a generic noun obtained from the indefinite description or from such a generic noun modified by adjectives or a restrictive relative clause obtained from what was predicated in the preceding sentence:

(9a) A man carne to the office today. The man tried to sell me an encyclopedia.

(9b) A man carne to the office today. The man who carne to the office today tried to sell me an encyclopedia.

(11) A man carne to the office today carrying a huge suitcase. It contained an encyclopedia.

(11a) A man carne to the office today carrying a huge suitcase. The suitcase contained an encyclopedia.

(11b) A man carne to the office today carrying a huge suitcase. The huge suitcase carried by the man who carne to the office contained an encyclopedia.

In some of these cases repetition of information makes the discourse sound like the awkward language of a children's first reader; the equivalences nevertheless hold.

There are several interesting features of this use of definite descriptions. One is that having used an indefinite description we immediately become entitled to use a definite description. This should give one pause before accepting the usual account of indefinite descriptions. In fact the usual account simply will not fit the use of the indefinite description here, as is suggested by trying to substitute for the initiating sentence in our examples one that explicitly asserts what that account says should be asserted:

(12)* At least one man carne to the office today. The man... (He...)

(13)* One or more men carne to the office today. The man... (He...)

The trouble seems to be that the pronoun or definite description in the second sentence can no longer have an anaphoric link with the first sentence.[14] If the sentences containing the indefinite description(s) in our examples do not assert merely that there is at least one thing having certain properties, nor obviously do they assert that there is exactly one thing having certain properties.

One would like to say that the initial sentences in these examples, the ones containing the indefinite description, serve to introduce a particular thing, a man, a suitcase, or whatever, and that this is what justifies the subsequent use of a pronoun or a definite description. But in what sense is a particular thing introduced?

One initially attractive idea is that the introducing sentence as a whole, not just the indefinite description, serves, if everything goes right, to identify an individual by providing a unique description. (It will be recalled that a subsequent definite description linked with the introducing sentence can be formed from the sentence as a whole by means of a restrictive relative clause—"The man who carne to the office...." from "A man carne to the office.") There are many cases in which this has plausibility. Sometimes the introducing sentence yields a description that by its very nature could be satisfied by one thing at most, as when the description contains a superlative or a definite ranking in some ordering:

(14) This set contains a least member. The least member of this set....

(15) A rank amateur carne in first in the Podunk Open today. The rank amateur who carne in first....

The speaker may assume certain background information available to the audience that would limit the things fitting the description to a single one:

(16) I believe she has a husband. He must be kind to her.

A background assumption that one can only have one husband (at a time) may operate. Finally, we may be able to view a speaker as sometimes implying (or asserting) that only one thing has the properties ascribed by the description:

(17) A loose connection is causing the hum in the television. The loose connection must be in the audio section.

But the problem is that in many cases we cannot suppose that the speaker believes or intends the description plus any background assumptions to pick out something uniquely. Our initial examples show this. (9), (9a), or (9b) might naturally begin an anecdote about an event at one's office told to friends who know little or nothing about what goes on there. Even if one used the fully expanded description, as in (9b), "A man carne to the office today. The man who carne to the office today tried to sell me an encyclopedia," the speaker is surely not committed to, nor does he intend to suggest that just one man carne to the office that day. Nor would he suppose that there are background assumptions shared by the audience that would allow them to recognize a particular man. There is a particular man presumably about which the speaker is talking, but that person is not identified by the descriptions used plus the circumstances of utterance. An introducing sentence, in fact, may supply no more than a generic noun:

(18) Once there was a king. The king rode a white horse.

This might begin a historical anecdote about a particular king. But which king is not determined by the descriptive content and the audience need not be presumed to have background assumptions that would narrow down the range.

Similar examples employing plural definite descriptions can easily be constructed:

(19) Some men carne to the office today. They wanted to sell me a philosophical computer.

(19a) Some men carne to the office today. The men....

Several groups of men may have come to the office today, although only one is being talked about. In suitable circumstances the speaker obviously may have no presumption that his audience can from any shared assumptions, contextual clues, etc., supply further qualifications that distinguish the group talked about from the others.

These occurrences of definite descriptions in very prosaic discourse fragments show, it seems to me, that by using the definite article a speaker need not be signaling any intention to "exhaust the range" of the description, as Vendler suggests, nor even to exhaust the range of an augmented description that his audience could be presumed to be capable of deriving from the context of utterance. Not only does this seem to show that Vendler's suggestion must be mistaken, but it indicates that the usual way of attempting to save a Russellian account of definite descriptions for ordinary discourse in the face of the indefiniteness of the descriptive content found so frequently cannot succeed either.

Yet in these examples some particular person or persons are being talked about and the definite descriptions and pronouns seem surely to have particular semantic referents. If the descriptive content of the uttered descriptions even augmented by background assumptions, etc., are insufficient to determine the referents, how is this possible? My answer will not be unexpected. The speaker having some person or persons in mind to talk about can provide the needed definiteness. Once more, then, we have a series of instances in which speaker reference appears necessary to provide semantic reference. Here, not just to provide the right reference, but to allow for reference at all.

VI

With the examples of the last section we have now considered two ways in which definite descriptions can be introduced into a discourse: they may simply appear *tout court,* as did Mr. Smith's "the fat old humbug we met yesterday," in which case they may be followed by pronouns apparently anaphorically linked to them; or they may appear after a sentence containing an indefinite description that in some fashion serves as an introduction, as in the examples of the last section. In the latter case they may be replaced by pronouns. In both cases we can distinguish between referential and attributive contexts depending upon whether or not there is speaker reference. But it may have been already noticed that there has been an important difference in the way in which I described the speaker's attitude toward his audience in referential contexts between the two. In the first part of the paper, where we were considering definite descriptions appearing *tout court* in a stretch of discourse, when there was speaker reference I said that the speaker intended his audience to recognize, partly by means of the description used, what his reference was to. And this, I believe, is a correct account, for instance, of the Mr. Smith example. But in the examples of the last section, where the definite description appears after an introducing sentence containing an indefinite description, the speaker need not be assumed to have any such intention toward his audience even where I claimed there was speaker reference. In telling the anecdote about what happened at the office beginning with "A man carne to the office today" and continuing, for example, with "The man...," the speaker need not expect nor intend his audience to recognize anyone as the subject of the story. What then makes such an example a case of speaker reference at all?

Of course I have argued that in such examples some particular person or thing is being talked about and the pronouns and definite descriptions that occur subsequent to the introducing sentence and linked with it seem surely to refer to that person or thing. But I believe we can put the point more precisely in terms of what the speaker intends concerning the truth conditions of his utterances: that he intends that truth or falsity shall be a function, in part, of the properties of the person or thing he has in mind.

Suppose that Woodward and Bernstein in their account of their investigation of the Nixon White House had said at a certain point:

(20) We now had a telephone call from a man high in the inner circle. He asked us to meet him at a certain suburban garage where he would give us confirmation of some of our conjectures. We later decided to give the man the code name "Deep Throat."[15]

Woodward and Bernstein never, of course, reveal to their readers who this high official is, and while some have tried to guess his identity and some may be certain of it, the authors did not intend that there should be recognition. The truth value of what they would have expressed in (20), however, depends upon the properties of the person they are writing about. Suppose that the man they had in mind did not ask them to meet him at a garage but at a certain bus stop. Then the second sentence in (20) expresses a falsehood. Suppose they never decided to give him the famous code name, but put this tidbit in the book because it seemed amusing. Then the third sentence expresses a falsehood.

Let us complicate this a bit by introducing a second mystery person. Suppose that the man that Woodward and Bernstein had in mind when writing the passage was not ever referred to by them as "Deep Throat," but that in fact they had given this code name to a second informant who entered into their investigations. So someone did possess the property attributed to "the man" in the third sentence. Still, I believe it is clear that that would not save the sentence from expressing a falsehood. The second informant was not being referred to here.

This determination of truth value by the properties of the speaker's referent extends also to the initiating sentence. If the man Woodward and Bernstein are writing about did not call them, but, say, left them a note in Woodward's copy of the *New York Times*, the first sentence in (20) would express a falsehood. And it would not be saved if some man high in the inner circles did in fact call them at the time in question.

We have then a distinction among the cases in which definite descriptions and pronouns anaphorically linked are preceded by an introducing sentence containing an indefinite description comparable to the referential/attributive distinction. The distinction rests on a notion of speaker reference, but one we were able to explicate in terms of the truth conditions of the utterances. It would be nice were we now able to do this across the board. The barrier in the way of giving such an account for definite descriptions introduced *tout court*, as in Geach's example of the conversation between the Smiths, however, is that we did not show in any conclusive fashion that the semantic reference of such a definite description is determined by the speaker's reference, when such exists, although we did, I believe, show that pronouns apparently anaphorically linked to it were. And to apply without further ado the present account of speaker reference would obviously beg the question. We have, however, been able in the last two sections to link speaker reference with the semantic reference of certain occurrences of definite descriptions, so these expressions are not slipping through our net altogether.

VII

A diesis to be found in somewhat different forms in both Chastain's and Vendler's essays would, if correct, allow us to apply the results of the last two sections directly to the case of definite descriptions introduced *tout court*. For both hold that the occurrence of definite descriptions in anaphoric chains initiated by a sentence containing an indefinite description is fundamental, and that when we find one introduced into a discourse apparently on its own hook, either it is not a genuine singular term or we should view it as derived from an understood, presupposed, or deleted initiating sentence containing an indefinite description. What we have been treating as two different sorts of cases are really not distinct.

If we accept their view, we could give the following sort of argument. Suppose, for example, that we are talking to someone we have reason to think will be able to single out a particular person we have in mind and we say:

(21) The man who carne to the office today tried to sell me an encyclopedia.

Now on the Vendler/Chastain view the definite description here really stands as a member of an anaphoric chain, the antecedent of which is either presupposed or in a covert discourse. The fully explicit discourse fragment from which this should be viewed as derived would be:

(22) A man carne to the office today. The man who carne to the office today tried to sell me an encyclopedia.

But we have already argued concerning (22) that the truth conditions of these utterances would depend upon the properties of the speaker's referent. We should therefore have to say the same thing about (21). And this, of course, would be directly contrary to the view represented at the beginning by Geach that speaker reference has nothing to do with the truth conditions of the utterance.

I am naturally not antagonistic toward the Vendler/Chastain view, but I am also not sure, aside perhaps for some considerations about simplicity and unification of the treatment of definite descriptions, that there is an argument that shows that the fundamental grammatical construction is that of a definite description anaphorically linked to an antecedent sentence containing an indefinite description. Nevertheless, I believe we can give something like the argument just mentioned.

First let me say something about how I view these two constructions—the definite description introduced *tout court* and the definite description anaphorically linked. In referential contexts, those where speaker reference is present, the choice of which construction to use is, I believe, a matter of the speaker's expectations and intentions toward his audience: does he expect and intend that they will recognize who or what he has in mind? If he does, then he will use a definite description with no further introduction; if not, he will begin with an introduction *via* an indefinite description. What the latter does, so to speak, is to announce that the speaker intends to speak about a particular thing or particular things following under a certain description—for example, he intends to speak of a particular king or a particular man or particular men who carne to the office. There is no implication in most cases that he will speak of everything falling under the description. Having done this, he can then go on to use a definite description or a pronoun to refer to what he wants to talk about. Where the speaker intends and expects his audience to be able to recognize what he speaks about from the description used (plus attendant circumstances), such an introduction is otiose. In fact, it would often be downright misleading because it would strongly suggest that the speaker did not believe his audience to be in a position to recognize this reference. Suppose we have just been talking to our colleague Joe who had with him an obviously close acquaintance. After they leave I say to you, "Joe's friend seemed a bit daffy." It would be no doubt obvious whom I was talking about. Had I said instead, however, "Joe has *a* friend. He seemed a bit daffy," I think you would be puzzled because my use of the introductory sentence suggests that you will not recognize my reference and that conflicts with the supposition that I am referring to a person we both have just met.

This account does not imply that the one construction is grammatically derived from the other, although it is consistent with that possibility. But if it does represent the difference between the two as far as why one might be used in some circumstances and the other in other circumstances, it also suggests that there should be no real difference in truth conditions or semantic references. Consider the indignant Mr. Smith again. Suppose he has two friends at the university, one of whom is a close confidant and familiar with the politics of the situation, the other of whom has just returned from a lengthy sabbatical in the nether regions of central Asia. To the second he says:

(23) A guy in the English Department has been getting chummy with the Dean. He, the guy in the English Department who has been chummy with the Dean, just got promoted to full professor. Shows what things have come to since you were away.

About such a case we argued that a particular person is being referred to but that the particularity cannot be expected to result from the descriptions actually employed applying to one person alone (the speaker may know full well that several members of the English Department have been getting chummy with the Dean), nor from background assumptions (the speaker does not expect that his newly returned colleague will possess facts that together with the speaker's descriptions will enable him to isolate a particular individual). Hence, we must go to the fact that the speaker has a particular person in mind, to speaker reference, to obtain the particularity. And it is properties of that individual that determine the truth or falsity of what the speaker uttered. Now to his more *au courant* colleague, the speaker might say,

(24) The guy in the English Department who has been getting chummy with the Dean has just gotten promoted to full professor. Shows what things are coming to.

In this sort of case we were able to argue that subsequent pronouns anaphorically linked with the definite description have as referent the speaker's referent. In particular, Smith's colleague might reply:

(25) You are wrong about him. I've investigated and he is far from chummy with the Dean—in fact they had a quarrel just last week.

And the pronouns here could hardly have as a referent whatever member of the English Department has been getting chummy with the Dean, since there is an explicit denial of that description.

But now if the only factor that affects Mr. Smith's shift from using an introductory indefinite description to introducing the definite description *tout court* is his expectation or lack of it about whether his audience will be able to recognize his reference, there can be no reason why the semantic facts about reference in the two cases should be different. And we can then, after all, apply the arguments that show semantic reference to be determined by speaker reference from the one sort of case to the other.

VIII

I have not touched upon the question of syntactic or semantic ambiguity. Are sentences containing definite descriptions that can be used in either referential or attributive contexts ambiguous? Are there two senses of the definite article? I have not done so in the first place because it seemed to me I could argue for the semantic significance of speaker reference and the referential/attributive distinction without, directly at any rate, tackling the problem of ambiguity. Secondly, the problem of ambiguity may require, for a solution, that another question I have put to one side, what it is to have something in mind, be answered first. And thirdly, we may need to work out more clearly than we have just what we mean to attribute when we speak of semantic or syntactic ambiguity, and that lies beyond the scope of this paper.

It might be thought, however, that if the position of this paper were correct that an ambiguity in the definite article would at least be suggested and that it is intuitively very implausible to suppose such an ambiguity. So that, until the question of ambiguity is resolved, a real doubt remains about whether that position can be correct. To this worry I will point out here that the situation of the definite article, given the position of this paper, remains in no worse shape in regards to ambiguity than several other operators and connectives in natural languages already are after philosophical scrutiny. We have already seen that sentences containing indefinite descriptions, while they may often be used to assert existential generalizations, are also used to introduce particular individuals, as in some of the examples in this paper where the sentence initiates an anaphoric chain. The same sort of worry about ambiguity should arise here. The "if... then______" construction provided another example. We know that such a construction (in the simplest form of declarative sentence) can be used to express what we might call a true conditional, but also can be used to assert the proposition expressed by the "consequent" where the "antecedent" expresses something like a condition the speaker presupposes for the asserted proposition to be of interest or significance in the circumstances. So I might tell someone to whom I am lending my car for a trip, "If it snows in the morning, there will be chains in the trunk." This might be used to assert a true conditional; I might, for example, be informing my audience that I will see to it that there are chains in the trunk on condition that I find it snowing in the morning. But I might also be asserting that there will be chains in the trunk, this being of interest, of course, only if it is snowing. (Similarly, Austin's "There are cookies in the cupboard, if you want some" would normally be taken as an assertion of the "consequent," but might be used by one's fairy godmother, who makes things true providing one wants them to be, to assert a true conditional.) I am not certain that just because of these data we should declare an ambiguity in the "if... then______" construction, although there certainly is a semantically interesting distinction to be drawn.

If we abstain from passing a ruling about ambiguity, can we draw any conclusions about the Russellian theory of definite descriptions? I am inclined to say that it cannot provide the proper analysis for the referential context in the sense of telling us what proposition is expressed. To fully sustain this would, I believe, require saying something more about what it is to have an individual in mind, for I can foresee the possibility of trying to obtain a Russellian proposition from descriptions in the speaker's mind. Let me then just say something about one way that may immediately occur to one attempting to obtain a Russellian proposition in the referential case.

The main problem brought up in the paper for a Russellian analysis in referential contexts was that of providing a unique denotation when neither speaker nor audience could be expected to believe that the description actually uttered was true of just one individual. It was argued that the usual way of trying to handle this problem—suggesting that the context of utterance would supply further distinguishing descriptions—would not in general work. It was at that point that we turned to what the speaker had in mind. But it might be thought that we could treat this as a special case of context supplying additional descriptions by supposing that what is implicit in such cases is just the additional description "which I, the speaker, have in mind," or some close approximation. In the Geach example, Mr. Smith could be represented as having said,

(26) The fat old humbug we met yesterday [and whom I have in mind] has just been made a full professor.

What occurs in brackets was not uttered by Mr. Smith, but intended to be supplied by the audience, Mrs. Smith, by its recognition of what Mr. Smith is up to. (26), in turn, would be analyzed, would be taken as expressing a proposition, along Russellian lines.

The problem I envisage with this suggestion is that it gives us the wrong proposition. The truth value of the Russellian proposition expressed by (26) would be partly a function of whom the speaker had in mind. If the Smiths met two fat old humbugs yesterday, one of whom got promoted and the other of whom did not, the Russellian proposition expressed by (26) would be true or false depending upon which Mr. Smith had in mind. But, I should like to say, whom Mr. Smith had in mind determines what proposition he expressed, not whether the proposition he expressed in any case is true or not. To put it shortly, while Mrs. Smith might say, "You could have prevented that by expressing your views to the committee," it would be absurd for her to say, "You could have prevented that by having someone else in mind."

Much more needs to be said, of course, about the topics mentioned in this last section. My aim, however, has been to argue that whatever the final view about them, we cannot divorce speaker reference from semantic reference.[16]

NOTES

1. The research for this paper was done in part under a grant from the National Endowment for the Humanities and while a Fellow at the Center for Advanced Study in the Behavioral Sciences.
2. "Reference and Definite Descriptions," *Philosophical Review* 75 (1966): 281–304 and "Putting Humpty Dumpty Together Again," *Philosophical Review* 77 (1968): 203–215.
3. *Reference and Generality* (Ithaca, 1962), p. 8.
4. Cf. Saul Kripke, "Naming and Necessity," in *Semantics of Natural Language*, eds. D. Davidson and G. Harmon (Dordrecht, 1972), fn. 3, p. 343.
5. As stated this is somewhat misleading. As will be seen in Section VI, I take such a speaker's intention toward his audience to be only a sufficient, not a necessary, condition for speaker reference.
6. "Reference and Context," *Language, Mind, and Knowledge*, ed. K. Gunderson, *Minnesota Studies in the Philosophy of Science*, Vol. VII (Minneapolis, 1975), pp. 194–269. As will be obvious, I am especially indebted to this essay.
7. "His smile is John's best feature," for example, is an instance where the determining member occurs later.
8. *Reference and Generality*, p. 124f.
9. "Reference and Context."
10. In this paper I use the term "reference" and variants on it in connection with definite descriptions both in referential contexts and in attributive. This is not

intended to imply that there may not be a big difference between the two situations, as "Reference and Definite Descriptions" suggested.

11. "Singular Terms," in *Linguistics in Philosophy* (Ithaca, 1967), Ch. 2.
12. "Singular Terms," pp. 50–51.
13. Chastain's view is that it is. He thus holds that "a man" in the first sentence of the discourse fragment would be a singular term with the same referent as the pronoun in the second. I am not wholly convinced of this. In some sense the first sentence introduces a particular person and, as I will argue, the truth value of what it expresses depends upon the properties of a particular man. I thus agree with Chastain that the sentence does not express an existential generalization of the sort we are often given as the reading of sentence containing indefinite descriptions. But I am not sure that that is enough to show that the indefinite description *itself* is a singular term. My reluctance stems from wondering whether it is not possible for a sentence to introduce, so to speak, an individual that subsequent pronouns refer to without itself containing an expression that refers to the individual. Perhaps the following would be such a case: "I had steak and lobster at Delmonico's before the play. It was a wonderful meal."
14. The anomaly of the preceding discourse fragments is not the main argument for the conclusion. That comes from a consideration of the truth conditions as will be seen later.
15. *All the President's Men* (New York, 1975). The example, of course, is not an actual quotation.
16. Too late for treatment in this paper, Saul Kripke's paper "Speaker Reference and Semantic Reference" (this volume, pp. 6–27) was published in *Midwest Studies in Philosophy* 2 (1977): 255–276. My paper was then in the final stages of production for a different publication (*Syntax and Semantics*, Vol. 9, edited by Peter Cole, Academic Press, 1978). The two papers now appear together in the present volume. I had heard a version of Kripke's paper given as a talk, but having no written copy to consult nor transcript of the talk, I did not want to rely on memory. Kripke's paper deals with the same topic as mine and comes to an apparently contrary conclusion, although I believe he is more concerned with the question of ambiguity than I have been here.

[6]

THE CONTINGENT *A PRIORI* AND RIGID DESIGNATORS

In "Naming and Necessity"[1] Saul Kripke describes the possibility of introducing a term for something, say a name for a person or a star, by citing a definite description, not to give a definitional equivalent, but solely to "fix the reference." A term so introduced will be a "rigid designator." Kripke calls "something a *rigid designator* if in any possible world it designates the same object...."[2] Kripke claims that as a consequence of this there is the startling possibility of knowing *a priori* contingent truths about the world. For suppose we propose to introduce the term "t" as the name of the denotation, if there is one, of the definite description "the ϕ." And we do not intend that "t" shall *mean* "the ϕ" or be a mere abbreviation for it. Rather, "t" is to designate whatever happens to be the ϕ; the definite description serves solely to fix the reference. If our procedure serves to introduce "t" as a rigid designator, "t" will designate the same entity in all possible worlds (in which it designates anything at all). It will designate the same thing that it does in this, the actual world. But there will be possible worlds in which what is the ϕ in the actual world, that which "t"

First published in *Midwest Studies in Philosophy*, 1977, **2**: 12–27.

designates, is not the ϕ in that world. Thus the statement that if the ϕ exists, t is the ϕ is merely contingently true, because there are possible worlds in which it is false. Yet, if the reference of "t" has been fixed solely by being the denotation of the description "the ϕ" it looks like it can be known *a priori* that if the ϕ exists, t is the ϕ.

This apparent result goes counter to the way philosophers have usually thought about what is knowable *a priori,* as Kripke would be the first to acknowledge.[3] If we offer as a somewhat vague explication of "knowable *a priori*" (and I will not attempt to give a sharper account) "knowable without recourse to experience" then perhaps some philosophers have considered certain statements to be both contingent and knowable *a priori;* perhaps, for example, the Cartesian *I exist* or some statements about language that can be known just through knowing the language. But the procedure Kripke is talking about is quite general and the statements that supposedly come out as both contingent and knowable a priori do not enjoy any special status such as the conclusion of the *Cogito* does. Here is one of his examples:

> An even better case of determining the reference of a name by description, as opposed to ostension, is the discovery of the planet Neptune. Neptune was hypothesized as the planet which caused such and such discrepancies in the orbits of certain other planets. If Leverrier indeed gave the name "Neptune" to the planet before it was ever seen, then he fixed the reference of "Neptune" by means of the description mentioned. At the Urne he was unable to see the planet even through a telescope. At this state, an a priori material equivalence held between the statements "Neptune exists" and "Some one planet perturbing the orbit of such and such other planets exists in such and such a position," and also such statements as "if such and such perturbations are caused by a planet, they are caused by Neptune" had the

> status of a priori truths. Nevertheless, they were not necessary truths, since "Neptune" was introduced as a name rigidly designating a certain planet. Leverrier could well have believed that if Neptune had been knocked off its course one million years earlier, it would cause no such perturbations and even that some other object might have caused the perturbations in its place.[4]

Before Kripke's discussion of the matter, most philosophers, I should think, would have considered the sentences he mentions, as they might be uttered by an astronomer today, as excellent paradigms of sentences expressing contingent truths knowable only *a posteriori*. As uttered by Leverrier, they would have said, the sentences might express truths knowable *a priori*, but that would have been because "Neptune," at the time, was a mere abbreviation for a certain description and the sentences expressed mere tautologies. Kripke would explain, at least in part, I believe, the failure of philosophers to consider the possibility of *a priori* contingent truths as, in the first place, a failure to keep firmly separate the epistemic distinction between the *a priori* and the *a posteriori* and the ontological distinction between the necessary and the contingent, the one defined in terms of knowability with or without recourse to experience and the other in terms of truth in possible worlds, and, in the second place, as a failure to make a distinction between establishing a term's meaning and fixing its reference. Whatever the extent of the influence of these factors there is another source of the uneasiness felt about the possibility of contingent *a priori* truths (I do not mean to suggest that Kripke would disagree). It might be put roughly as follows: If a truth is a contingent one then it is made true, so to speak, by some actual state of affairs in the world that, at least in the sorts of examples we are interested in, exists independently of our language and our linguistic conventions. How can we become aware of such a truth, come to know the existence of such a state of affairs, merely by performing an act of linguistic stipulation? Or, to put it another way, contingent truths are true in only a proper subclass of all possible worlds; how by a mere stipulation of how the reference of a term is to be fixed, can we come to know that our world is a member of that subclass?

I share these philosophical qualms and yet at the same time I believe that Kripke has described a viable procedure for introducing a term as a rigid designator (viable in theory; as will become clear I am dubious that it can be shown to be a part of our usual linguistic practices). My way out of this dilemma in this paper will be to suggest that the procedure does not have the consequence claimed for it; it does not in fact yield the possibility of knowing *a priori* contingent truths.

I

I should first say something, I believe, about the question of whether or not a name can be introduced as a rigid designator, as opposed to a mere abbreviation, by using a definite description. Michael Dummett, in his long discussion of Kripke's work in his recent book *Frege: Philosophy of Language*,[5] seems to want to challenge this. In discussing this it is important to be quite sure what we are asking. In particular, we must separate the factual issue of whether it is part of our actual practice ever to introduce names in this way from the theoretical issue of whether names could be introduced in this way. Kripke does sometimes talk about examples, such as the introduction of the name "Neptune" by Leverrier, as if he wanted to assert that the example is one in which a name has been introduced as a rigid designator. And he may give the impression that he even has an argument that shows that this is so. (I believe Dummett so reads him.) It is one thing to fault him on these counts, if indeed those were his intentions, and quite another to show that there is something theoretically wrong with the very notion of introducing a name in that way. It seems to me that the philosophical worry about the possibility of knowledge *a priori* of contingent truths should be just as strong if it is no more than a theoretical possibility that a name should be introduced in such a way as to allow for such knowledge.

It is, of course, of importance whether or not names are ever introduced as rigid designators by the use of definite descriptions to fix their reference. The philosophically interesting question is, what would show that that was what had been done as opposed to introducing the name as an abbreviation for the description? For we should not, of course, suppose that names *cannot* be introduced as abbreviations; it is obvious that we can do that if we want to. Leverrier probably did not say anything that would disclose an intention that the name should function one way rather than the other. Kripke tells us that this is an example of the introduction of a name as a rigid designator, but why is he so confident that it is not an example of a name introduced as an abbreviation? At the end of the passage quoted he may seem to be giving an argument. He says, of the things he believes Leverrier could know *a priori*:

> Nevertheless, they were not *necessary* truths, since "Neptune" was introduced as a name rigidly designating a certain planet. Leverrier could well have believed that if Neptune had been knocked off its course one million years earlier, it would cause no such perturbations and even that some other object might have caused the perturbations in its place.[6]

It might be thought that there is the following sort of argument being given: Take the modal sentence,

(A) Neptune might have existed and not been the cause of the perturbations in the orbit of Uranus.[7]

Following Kripke, it seems that having just introduced the name *via* the description contained in (A), Leverrier might nevertheless believe without any inconsistency what (A) expresses. But that seems to show that the following sentence expresses a contingent truth:

(B) If Neptune exists, Neptune is the cause of the perturbations in the orbit of Uranus.

But if "Neptune" were a mere abbreviation for the description in question then (B) would be equivalent, by substitution of the description for the name, to a mere tautology. Thus, or so it might seem, we can show that "Neptune" was not introduced as an abbreviation.

Anyone bent on maintaining that in Kripke's example the name was introduced as an abbreviation can escape this argument. He will, as Dummett does, point to scope differences. Let us suppose that "Neptune" was introduced as an abbreviation for the description. Then we can explain why we are inclined to agree with Kripke that Leverrier might without inconsistency believe what (A) expresses by claiming that (A) is ambiguous as between two readings, one with the modal operator having wide scope and the other with its having narrow scope. That is, if we substitute for "Neptune" in (A) its claimed definitional equivalent we obtain:

(C) The cause of the perturbations in the orbit of Uranus might have existed and not been the cause of the perturbations in the orbit of Uranus.

But this, it would be claimed, is ambiguous. We can represent the two readings explicitly by:

(D) It might have been the case that [the cause of the perturbations in the orbit of Uranus did not cause the perturbations in the orbit of Uranus].

and

(E) The cause of the perturbations in the orbit of Uranus might have been such that it did not cause the perturbations in the orbit of Uranus.

(D), of course, is plainly false and we cannot suppose that Leverrier would have believed it. But (E) expresses something he should have believed, for surely, the planet actually responsible for the perturbations might have met with an accident millions of years ago, etc.

That Leverrier might well have consistently believed what is expressed by (A) does not then show that "Neptune" was not introduced by him as an abbreviation for the description nor that (B) is contingently true. For on the hypothesis that it was introduced as an abbreviation (E) expresses one of the propositions (A) could express and (E) is something Leverrier might well have believed.

The attempt to construct an argument from modal beliefs to show that a rigid designator has been introduced seems, then, always open to this sort of evasion. As I will emphasize once more a bit later, however, this does not show in the least that names cannot be introduced as rigid designators by means of definite descriptions, much less that there is, for example, anything wrong with the thesis that names are, in general, rigid designators.

If we were concerned to know about an actual case whether a name had been introduced, by means of a description, as a rigid designator rather than as an abbreviation, I am inclined to believe we would be in some difficulty. Not only is there no conclusive argument of the sort described, I doubt that we could rely in general on linguistic intuitions. In the absence of an explicit stipulation that the name shall be taken as a rigid designator and the description as merely fixing the reference (and historically we have not, I believe, possessed a formula for making such a stipulation[8]) we would have to rely on our intuitions about the syntactic, semantic, modal or epistemic properties of sentences in which the introduced name occurs. The two possibilities, that the name is a rigid designator and that it is abbreviation, yield different predictions concerning the properties of various sentences and classes of sentences. For example, if the name is a rigid designator then, where "N" is the introduced name and "the ϕ" the introducing description, the sentence of the following form would express a contingent truth:

(F) If N exists, then N is the ϕ.

If, on the other hand, the name is an abbreviation the sentence of that form would express a tautology. But this difference in the predicted status of a certain sentence does not seem to me to be a *usable* difference. In the absence of an explicit stipulation, any profession of an intuition about the status that we might make or even that the stipulator himself might make would seem to have the same status as Kripke's opinion that the sentence, in certain examples, expresses a contingent truth or Dummett's, about the same examples, that it does not. For my own part, when I think about such an example as the "Neptune" case, I don't find myself with any strong intuition one way or the other.

The same unusability of differences in predicted properties seems to me to hold for other sentence types. If the name is an abbreviation, it follows that certain pairs of sentences will be paraphrases of each other, and that would not be the case if the name is a rigid designator. Thus, in the "Neptune" example, "Neptune is a large planet" would be paraphrasable, if the name is an abbreviation for the description, as "The cause of the perturbations in the orbit of Uranus is a large planet." When I think of Leverrier introducing the name by saying some such thing as "Let us call the cause of the perturbations in the orbit of Uranus 'Neptune,' " I do not find myself with any strong intuitions that such pairs of sentences are or are not paraphrases of each other. Similarly, as we saw, modal sentences such as (A) in the argument discussed above, will have two non-equivalent readings if the name has been introduced as an abbreviation, but not if it is a rigid designator. Where "N" is a rigid designator to say "It might have been the case that [N is not ϕ]" is equivalent to saying "N might have been such that it is not ϕ" (this point is sometimes put by saying that the name always has wide scope—that it can always be brought outside the scope of the modal operator without change of meaning). But again I doubt that anyone would have any strong intuitions about this concerning a situation such as that of Leverrier and the introduction of the name "Neptune"—at least none not motivated by a theory about the matter.

I believe the conclusion to be drawn from this is that in the absence of stipulation that the name shall be one or the other, it would be indeterminate whether a name introduced by means of a description is a rigid designator or an abbreviation, so long as the name continues to be pegged to the description. It may be interesting that a name could have this indeterminacy, but I do not see that it should cause concern. It certainly would not make any practical difference.

It will be indeterminate, for example, whether certain pairs of sentences are paraphrases of each other, but there will not be any question but that what they express will have the same truth value. And should someone wonder how we know this, the right response would be to remind him of the agreed upon stipulation, even though it is indeterminate whether or not that stipulation introduced a rigid designator or an abbreviation. This conclusion, of course, presupposes that the concept of introducing a name as a rigid designator by means of a description is a coherent one.

It seems to me that the concept *is* a coherent one. If it is specifically intended and stipulated that this introduction of a name is to be the introduction of a rigid designator, I see no theoretical reason to suppose that the stipulation cannot accomplish what is intended. Certainly none of the above facts about the status of names in cases where there is no explicit intention one way or the other casts any shadow on the theoretical possibility of such an introduction. (And I must confess that while I am not confident I fully grasp Dummett's attack on Kripke, a large part of it seems to me to accomplish no more than what I have set out above.) I should like also to point out even more emphatically that these facts certainly cast no doubt upon the thesis that in general names are rigid designators. For we are talking now about a special sort of situation, one in which a name is introduced by and subsequently, for some period of time, is pegged to a definite description. And there is no obvious reason why what we would conclude about this sort of situation should be extended to or have implications for what we should say about, say, the present use of the names "Aristotle" or "Ford." Those who hold that such names are rigid designators need not hold that they are now or were at any time pegged to a definite description that "fixes the referent." A name such as "Neptune," which we will suppose was first introduced by some description, is certainly no longer tied to the description that was used to introduce it. This is shown by the fact that if someone were to ask an astronomer how he knows that Neptune causes the perturbations in the orbit of Uranus, he would be treated, undoubtedly, to a discussion of such things as astronomical observations, details of orbits, gravitational forces and the like, whereas, just after Leverrier's stipulation the same question would have received (whatever the name's status as rigid designator or abbreviation) some such reply as "That is just what we call 'Neptune' " or "It is just by stipulation that we call the cause of those perturbations, 'Neptune.'" Now those who hold some version of what I have called the "principle of identifying descriptions,"[9] a view that Kripke and I have attacked, will describe the breaking away of the name from the introducing description either as a case in which it has come to be an abbreviation for (or associated with, to accommodate certain versions) another description or as the introducing description having come to be merely one member of a set of descriptions associated with the name (where the referent is determined by being that which satisfies some proportion of the descriptions). But there is no obvious reason why someone who held that the name had originally been introduced as a rigid designator by means of one description should have to say that now, when it has been disengaged from that description, there is some *other* description that "fixes" its referent.[10] And in fact those who hold that a name such as "Neptune" is currently a rigid designator do not take, so far as I know, any such route. Instead, they theorize that there is another relationship that can hold between the user(s) of a name, the name and the thing named in virtue of which the thing *is* named and that does not involve the thing satisfying any descriptions associated with the name. Thus Kripke speaks of a causal relationship, I have talked about a relationship of being involved in an historical explanation of the use of a name[11] and David Kaplan introduced a technical notion of a name being a name *of* something for someone, characterized in terms of how the user acquired the name.[12] A name that functions according to some version of such a theory will be a rigid designator, but not in virtue of there being some definite description associated with the name that fixes the reference. If any such theory is tenable, then what we say about the situation, for example, when "Neptune" was tied to a description, will not have any immediate application, at any rate, to the situation after it has become divorced from the introducing description. Thus, where there has been no explicit stipulation that a name being introduced via a description shall be construed as a rigid designator, the fact that there is no argument that would show that it is a rigid designator nor, as I have suggested, the possibility of firm intuitions that might point that way, neither demonstrates (at least straight off) anything wrong with the thesis that names in general are rigid designators nor even that there is anything amiss with the notion of introducing rigid designators by description. As for the latter, we will from now on suppose that the stipulation that the name shall be a rigid designator and the introducing description a device for fixing the reference is explicitly made. Whether or not we in fact would have any practical reason for doing this, rather than leaving the matter indeterminate, the theoretical possibility that a consequence would be knowledge *a priori* of contingent truths must be faced.

II

About Kripke's view that by the sort of stipulative introduction of a name as a rigid designator one would thereby be in a position to know a contingent truth *a priori,* Dummett remarks, "Counter-intuitive it undoubtedly is, but it appears to follow from Kripke's arguments: something must, therefore, be amiss with those arguments."[13] I am not sure what he meant by "those arguments," but I do want to question whether it follows from the possibility of introducing a rigid designator by means of a description that certain contingent truths are knowable *a priori*. And I will suggest that it does not. (Or, more cautiously, if there are thereby any contingent truths knowable *a priori* they will not be of the sort Kripke mentions and will not cause the philosophical qualms mentioned at the beginning.) In doing this I am going to invoke a distinction between knowing that a certain sentence expresses a truth and knowing the truth of what is expressed by the sentence. I am going to suggest that as the result of the introduction of a name as a rigid designator by means of a description fixing the referent we can come to know, perhaps even *a priori*, that certain sentences express truths, but we do not come to know, *a priori*, the truth of what they express.[14] This may turn out to sound as paradoxical as Kripke's position on the matter, but at least it will not be for the same reasons.

We can illustrate the distinction I have in mind, in the first place, by a familiar kind of example. A person could know that a certain sentence expresses a truth if he has been told by an unimpeachable source that it does. Thus I could learn from a German-speaking friend that a certain German sentence expresses something true, but if I do not speak German and do not know what the sentence means I would say that I do not know the truth of what the sentence expresses—or rather, if by chance I do, it would not be just from the information given me by my friend. Similarly, I could be assured by a qualified mathematician that a certain mathematical sentence expresses a theorem, without thereby knowing the truth of the theorem expressed, if I am ignorant of what the mathematical sentence means. Now it is true that in such cases I can pass on to someone else not only that the sentence in question expresses a truth, but also the truth it expresses. For example, having read in an authoritative article in *Scientific American*, "The oblateness of Mars is .003," I may be said to know that that sentence expresses a truth, but if I have not the foggiest idea of what is meant by "oblateness," I do not think I can be said to know that the oblateness of Mars is .003. Yet if I subsequently happen to be in a group discussing the properties of the planets and someone asks what the oblateness of Mars is, I might answer "It is .003." But I think I act here, to use an apt expression of Gareth Evans,[15] as a mere mouthpiece, passing on a statement about matters of which *I* am ignorant.

In these sorts of examples the person is ignorant of the meaning of at least part of the sentence involved. Where demonstratives or pronouns are involved, however, one might know, at least in one ordinary sense, what a sentence means, know that it expresses something true, but not know the truth of what it expresses. If you say to me, "That is mine," I know what the sentence means and if, for example, I also know that you keep scrupulous track of your possessions, but never claim something that is not yours, I may know that the sentence, on this occasion of its use, expresses something true. But if I fail to grasp what it is that you are referring to by "that" I will not yet know the truth of what the sentence, on this occasion, expresses.

None of this, of course, is new; I mention these examples only to make sure the distinction I want is clear. A slightly more interesting example and one somewhat closer to the situation which, I will suggest, holds in the case of introducing rigid designators via descriptions, is suggested by a remark of William Kneale's (quoted by Kripke for another purpose). Kneale says, "While it may be informative to tell a man that the most famous Greek philosopher was called Socrates, it is obviously trifling to tell him that Socrates was called Socrates."[16] As Kripke points out Kneale cannot be correct about the example as he gives it, because it is surely not trifling to tell someone that Socrates *was* called "Socrates"—it is not even obviously true that Socrates had the same name we use for him. But let us patch this up and suppose that someone says, "Socrates is called by me 'Socrates.'" This looks more like it may be trifling and let us grant that it is. Then in general if anyone says something of the form "N is called by me 'N,'" he will have asserted something trifling, if he asserts anything at all. Now suppose that you say to me "Vladimir is called by me 'Vladimir'" and I do not have the least idea who Vladimir is. From the general principle I can see that if you have asserted anything, your sentence expresses a truth. But I do not believe that I know that Vladimir is called "Vladimir" by you. I do not know the truth of what your sentence expresses. This example shows that considerations other than the reliable testimony of those who understand what a sentence expresses can put one in the position of knowing that a sentence expresses a truth, but not knowing the truth of what it expresses.

III

If we imagine all the participants to have mastered the notion of a rigid designator then we could make explicit the intention to introduce a name as a rigid designator by using some such formula as, "Let 'N' be a rigid designator with its referent fixed by 'the ϕ.'" But, because I think it somewhat illuminating to do it this way, I am going to propose instead that we think of the introduction as consisting of stipulating that a certain sentence shall express a contingent truth. If we want to introduce the name "N" by means of the description of "the ϕ" then the formula we would use would be:

(a) Provided that the ϕ exists, let "N is the ϕ" express a contingent truth.

It is a condition on the stipulation that the ϕ exists and should it turn out that it does not, the stipulation, we might say, has been an unhappy one and not to be taken as being in effect.[17] It should be clear from the preceding remarks that I am not in any way suggesting that this represents some sort of analysis of any practice that we have ever engaged in.

No doubt the procedure looks strange. We are accustomed to linguistic conventions that give meaning to words, phrases and sometimes whole sentences, but not to conventions that specify that a certain sentence shall express a truth. Perhaps the closest approximation in ordinary practice is the laying down of axioms in an axiom system. But, of course, what is most strange about the procedure is that a sentence is by stipulation to express a contingent truth.

I can imagine a philosophical worry about the procedure not unlike the worry about the possibility of the contingent *a priori*. How, it might be asked, could one *stipulate* that something be contingently true? What makes something contingently true is how the world is, the existence or non-existence of some state of affairs. Surely only God, if even He, could perform the miracle of stipulating how the world shall be.

How shall we reply to this? In the first place, it is of course crucial that the name in the sentence about which the stipulation is made is a fresh new name or, if it has been used previously to name something, that it is being given a new use. I could not, for example, get away with stipulating that, say, "Gerald Ford will be starting quarterback for the Rams in 1976," where I intend all the words to have their usual meanings and the names their usual referents, shall be contingently true. Secondly, the philosophical worry assumes that we are trying by mere stipulation to establish that a certain state of affairs shall exist. That *would* be an exceedingly odd thing to suggest we try to do. But that is not what the stipulation is intended to accomplish nor does it do so. It stipulates that a certain sentence containing a name for which there is no independently intended referent shall express a contingent truth. Now what state of affairs will turn out, if any does, to correspond to the sentence is, so to speak, up to the world. Imagine the detective, of philosophical bent, instead of using the hackneyed, "Let us call the murderer 'X,'" saying "Provided the murderer exists, let 'Vladimir is the murderer' express a contingent truth." We can suppose that Jones is the actual murderer. So in the actual world the state of affairs that corresponds to the sentence in question is Jones being the murderer and what the sentence expresses is the existence of that state of affairs. But someone else might have been *the* murderer; in other possible worlds it is Smith or Robinson. We can imagine everything being the same except that someone else is the murderer (and whatever differences are entailed by that). Then a different state of affairs would correspond to the sentence and it would express the existence of a different state of affairs. We could also put this by saying that in different possible worlds "Vladimir," as the name is introduced by the stipulation in those worlds, would turn out to rigidly designate someone else. So the detective is not, by stipulation, attempting to create a state of affairs (other than a linguistic one).

Not only does the detective not create, by stipulation, any state of affairs (other than a linguistic one), but I should like to say nor does he thereby come to know the existence of any state of affairs. Kripke himself says, in connection with his example of the standard meter bar, "But, merely by fixing a system of measurement, has he thereby *learned* some (contingent) information about the world, some *new fact* that he did not know before? It seems plausible that in some sense he did not, though it is undeniably a contingent fact that S is one meter long."[18] I should like to question, in these cases, whether there is *any* sense in which by the sort of stipulation we are talking about a person could come to know something of which he was previously ignorant.

Let us look at an example from David Kaplan's paper "Quantifying In" which he also uses in a subsequent paper "Dthat,"[19] and about which, interestingly, he draws diametrically opposite conclusions, a fact I will touch upon later. I will adapt the example slightly to fit the format we are using. Consider the description, "the first child born in the 21st century." Even though the denotation, if there is one, does not yet exist and moreover, with certain assumptions about determinism and freedom of the will, it may not even now be determined who that individual will be, we can by stipulation introduce a rigid designator for that person, if there is to be one. So, following Kaplan, we shall stipulate that providing the first child born in the 21st century will exist, the sentence "Newman 1 will be the first child born in the 21st century" shall express a contingent truth. Let us now imagine that just after midnight on New Century's Eve a child is born who is firmly established to be the first born of the century. He is baptized "John," but those of us who are still around, remembering our stipulation, also call this child "Newman 1." Now it seems to me that it would be outrageous to say that some twenty-five years or so before his birth, we knew that John would be the first child born in the 21st century. Suppose one of us, living to a ripe old age, were to meet John after he has grown up a bit. Would it be true to say to John, "I call you 'Newman 1' and Newman 1, I knew some twenty-five years or so before your birth that you would be the first child born in the 21st century"?

The Neptunians are watching on their interplanetary videoscope; they see and hear Leverrier perform his act of stipulation (and since this is science fiction let us also imagine that, anachronistically, he intends the name he is introducing to be a rigid designator and even uses our formula). They know that their planet is the cause of the perturbations in the orbit of Uranus. Would they be justified in concluding that the Earthling has learned or come to know that their planet is the cause? It seems to me that the answer is obviously that they would not. Suppose they call their planet "Enutpen." Would they be justified in saying, in Enutpenese, that the Earthling now knows that Enutpen is the cause of those perturbations? Again I think not. Suppose, finally, that they like the sound of the name "Neptune"; one of them suggests they too adopt the Earthlings' convention and agree that "Neptune ______" (where "______" is a translation into Enutpense of "is the cause of the perturbations in the orbit of Uranus") shall express a contingent truth. Would they be justified in saying that the Earthling knows the truth of what is expressed by them as "Neptune ______"? I am still inclined to say that they would not be.

The above are supposed to be considerations toward showing that what some of us may know after the advent of the 21st century is not anything we know now and that what the Neptunians may have known is not anything that Leverrier knew just as a result of his stipulation. And I am assuming that if we know something now just as a result of our stipulation it cannot be anything different from something we may know after the birth of the first child in the 21st century and that if Leverrier did know something just as the result of his stipulation it could not be different from what the Neptunians knew.

I am assuming, to use the jargon, that if we now have any knowledge (other than about linguistic matters) just as a result of the stipulation concerning the sentence, "Newman 1 will be the first child born in the 21st century" it would have to be knowledge *de re*. That is, it would have to be knowledge *about* an individual in the sense that there is (or will be) an individual about whom we now know something and if that individual turns out to be John we now know something about John. We could, of course, put this point by saying that the sentence which expresses the proposition that we have such knowledge, and which contains the name "Newman 1" is open to substitution on the name and allows of existential generalization on it. This is as opposed to the knowledge we might come to have *de dicto*, for example, that the firstborn child, if there will be one, in the 21st century will be bald, knowledge that we might come to have, for example, because we get indisputable evidence that pollution from aerosol sprays has caused genetic changes and every child born after a certain time will be bald. That knowledge would not be knowledge *about* a certain individual, not knowledge about John.

I make this assumption that the knowledge, if we have it, would have to be *de re* not simply on the grounds that "Newman 1" is a rigid designator. It does not follow from the fact that a term is a rigid designator that when it enters into a statement of propositional attitude, the attitude ascribed must be *de re*. It does not follow because not all rigid designators lack descriptive content. Mathematical definite descriptions, when they do not lack a denotation, presumably would be rigid designators, designating the same thing in all possible worlds. Although I know that the 98th prime number is not divisible by three, it does not follow that I know about the number which is the 98th prime number that is not divisible by three.[20] It is rather, then, that as these stipulations introduce names they give the names no descriptive content that leads me to say that the knowledge, if there is any, must be *de re* knowledge and then to try to show that we do not have such *de re* knowledge.

Now the notion of *de re* propositional attitudes is a notoriously difficult one. It is difficult to know what the proper analysis is of statements ascribing such attitudes and it is difficult to know under what conditions they are true. It also creates formidable problems for the sort of theory of reference to which Kripke and I and others subscribe, problems that have to do with identity conditions for such propositional attitudes.[21] I do not want to push the whole matter under the rug, but I would like, if possible, to step around the messy areas for the purposes of the point I want to establish in this paper.

Putting aside any attempt to account for them and any theories about how names function, let us look at a couple of loose principles concerning names and propositional attitudes. I say "loose" because I do not want to defend them as having no counter-examples.[22] The first one is this: If an object is called by one name, say "N," by one group of people and by another name by a second group, say "M," and if, in the language of the first group "N is ϕ" expresses a bit of knowledge of theirs and if "is ψ" is a translation of "is ϕ" into the language of the second group then if the relevant facts are known to the second group, they can say truly that the first group "knew that M is ψ." Thus, for example, our historians would say that the early Indian residents knew that Santa Catalina is a single island, unlike the first Spanish explorers in the area, even though, of course, the Indians have a different name for it. Now this principle fails in the "Newman" and "Neptune" examples. If the first child born in the 21st century comes to be named "John" it would not be correct to say then that although we had a different name for him we knew twenty-five years beforehand that John would be the first child born in the 21st century. Nor should the Neptunians admit that while Leverrier, presuming he has introduced a name as a rigid designator, had a different name for Enutpen, he knew that Enutpen was the cause of the perturbations in the orbit of Uranus.

Another such principle is this: If one has a name for a person, say "N," and there is a bit of knowledge that one would express by saying "N is ϕ" then if one subsequently meets the person it will be true to say to him, using the second-person pronoun, "I knew that you were

ϕ." I believe I knew that Bertrand Russell was a short man. Had I met him I could quite correctly, though impolitely, say to him, "I knew that you were a short man." As we have seen this too fails in the "Newman 1" case. (A similar loose principle could be constructed substituting a demonstrative such as "this planet" that would be seen as failing in the "Neptune" example.)

In the absence of any other explanation of why these principles should fail in these cases I suggest that the reason is that the stipulations have not given rise to any knowledge (other than of linguistic matters). And so not to any knowledge *a priori.*

IV

If this is correct that indeed the introduction of a rigid designator by a definite description does not give rise to the sort of knowledge Kripke thought would be *a priori* and of contingent truths, what then of the argument at the beginning that seemed to show that it would? Where does it go wrong? The crucial step, I believe, was where we said, "Yet, if the referent of 't' has been fixed solely by being the denotation of the definite description 'the ϕ' it looks like it can be known *a priori* that provided the ϕ exists, t is the ϕ." I believe that this move looks very plausible because what *can,* I believe, be known is the following:

(A) Provided the ϕ exists, "t is the ϕ" expresses a contingent truth.

I am supposing here that (A) is not itself the stipulation, even though it is close to it in phrasing, but a statement about the language into which the name has been introduced. But it does not follow from the fact that as the result of a stipulation one can know something of the form of (A) that one thereby knows the truth of what the sentence of the following form expresses:

(B) Provided the ϕ exists, t is the ϕ.

But, of course, it was the truth of what some sentences of form (B) express that Kripke thought we could know *a priori* as the result of a stipulation.

Now it might be asked whether we have not still got the contingent *a priori* on our hands, because does not (A) express a contingent truth, albeit one about a language, and will it not be knowable *a priori*? My answer to this is that I am not sure whether in the circumstances what sentences of form (A) express are both contingent and *a priori*. But if they are they are harmless varieties of the contingent *a priori*, examples of which we could produce without recourse to stipulations introducing rigid designators. Perhaps it would be argued that since such sentences express a truth about a language that might have been false (if, for example, the stipulation had not been made) they are contingent and that because their truth can be assured merely by reference back to a linguistic stipulation, they are *a priori*. But if so, then, for example, traditional definitions will yield the contingent *a priori*. Suppose I stipulate that "Widgit" shall mean by definition "green cow," then I know the truth of what the following expresses:

(C) Provided there are any green cows, "Widgits are green cows" expresses a truth.

But the same considerations would argue for this being *a priori* knowledge of a contingent truth. If this proves that there can be *a priori* knowledge of the contingent, then it seems to me that the contingent *a priori* is not very scary and not very interesting.

V

At the end of his paper "Dthat" Kaplan says that "It is now clear that I can assert to the first child to be born in the 21st century that *he* will be bald." In terms of the modifications in the example made in this paper, he thinks he could do this, having introduced the name "Newman 1" in the way specified, by "assertively uttering" "Newman 1 will be bald." Kaplan is here recanting the position he had in "Quantifying In." Part of the task Kaplan set for himself in that paper was to give the conditions under which a person can correctly be said to have a *de re* propositional attitude. The "Newman 1" example was, in fact, used to show the necessity of requiring for such an attitude that the person having it be in a special sort of relationship to the entity about which he has it. He says, "I am unwilling to adopt any theory of proper names which permits me to perform a dubbing in absentia, as by solemnly declaring 'I hereby dub the first child to be born in the twenty-second century "Newman 1."' "[23] In "Dthat" he has become armed with the apparatus for introducing rigid designators and definite descriptions and this leads him, I believe, to think that he can perform the feat that he earlier thought obviously impossible. If the position of this paper is correct, however, the fact that a name is introduced as a rigid designator does not by itself put a person in a position to have *de re* propositional attitudes toward the entity rigidly designated. For essentially the same considerations that were adduced for denying that there was knowledge of an entity just in virtue of the sort of stipulation that introduces a rigid designator by means of a description can be applied to the other propositional attitudes. It would, for example, seem to me just as incorrect to say to John who turns out to be the first child born in the 21st century, "I believed about you some twenty-five years before your birth ... ," "I asserted about you some twenty-five years before your birth ... ," etc.

If this is so, we are in the somewhat odd position of possessing a mechanism for introducing a name that rigidly designates something, but a mechanism that is not powerful enough to allow us to use the name! But that it is odd does not show, of course, that it is not true.

Still it may be thought that the result is so odd that something must be wrong. It might be said, "I can understand how a person might know about a sentence in someone else's language or idiolect that it expresses a truth without knowing the truth of what it expresses; even where the sentence is in some sense, a sentence in your language, as in the examples employing demonstratives or proper names as used by someone else, at least the reference has been fixed by the other person and that is why you might know that the sentence, as used by him, expresses a truth without knowing the truth of what it expresses. But you are trying to tell us that there is a procedure for introducing a name, with its reference fixed, and thereby an indefinite number of sentences employing the name, into your very own language. And that is what makes it difficult to see how, concerning some of these sentences introduced into your language, you could be in the position of knowing that they express truths, but not knowing the truth of what they express. In particular, if 'P' is a sentence in your language and we assume that the reference of any names and demonstratives has also been fixed, how could you fail to know that 'P' expresses a truth if and only if P? But, of course, if you know that in the cases you are concerned about, you will know the truth of what is expressed."

I will, of course, have to agree that if I am right one result of introducing names via definite descriptions in the way suggested is that there are sentences introduced into one's language such that about any particular one "P," one does not know that "P" expresses a truth if and only if P. Or, rather, I will if this is not simply a terminological dispute—simply a refusal on the one side to say that a sentence has been introduced into a person's language unless he knows the biconditional. In that case, I do not mind what we say, as Anscombe, I believe, once put it, so long as the facts of the matter are straight. And the facts, as I have described them, are that the procedure sets up the apparatus necessary for a set of sentences to express truths and falsehoods without thereby putting the possessor of the apparatus in a position to know what they express. And the real issue, I believe, is whether there is any impossibility in this. If we admit the possibility, then whether or not we say that the sentences have really been introduced into his language is unimportant. Consider the following analogous situation: I close my eyes and say (pointing), "I will call the color of that 'Murple.'" I do not know what I am pointing to, if anything. Let us suppose I am pointing to something of a definite color. Have I not set up an indefinite number of sentences, for example, "Murple is the color of my true love's hair," each of which expresses something true or false? But while my eyes remain shut I do not believe I know what they express. The apparatus, however, has been constructed and I have only to open my eyes to see, for example, how ludicrous it would be to think that murple is the color of my true love's hair and that grass is murple. And analogously to the introduction of names by the procedure we have been talking about, I believe I know, while my eyes are shut, that providing I am pointing to something of a definite color, where were I to use assertively the sentence "Murple is the color of that" with eyes open, I would express a truth, but with eyes closed I do not believe I would know the truth of what I would have asserted.

There is, however, an alternative way of characterizing the situation that I do not know how, at the moment, to counter.[24] And that is that what these stipulations succeed in doing is reserving a name for a future use. Thus "Newman 1" is now reserved for use in referring to whoever turns out to be the first child born in the 21st century, much as prospective parents may choose a name for the next female child they have. When we come to know who the first child born in the 21st century is, when we come to be in a position to refer to him and have beliefs about him, then the name, if we remember and adhere to our former intentions, becomes a part of our repertoire and an indefinite number of sentences using the name enter our language. A consequence of this account is that these sentences did not express anything true or false prior to the time at which we were in a position to use them ourselves. And thus it would be wrong to characterize our position as that of knowing that certain sentences express truths, but not knowing the true of what they express. Rather, what we can know is that certain sentences, if and when we come to be in a position to use them, *will* express truths.

I do not, at the moment, see how to show that this way of viewing the matter, as opposed to how I have described it, is or is not the correct way. I do not, however, find this particularly upsetting. The alternative view still preserves the main points I wish to make, namely, that there is a way of introducing a name, albeit as a reserved name, *via* a definite description, but not as an abbreviation, and that knowledge a priori of contingent truths (of a kind to raise philosophical qualms) is not a result.

VI

In "Quantifying In," Kaplan held that in order to have a *de re* propositional attitude toward an entity one must be, as he put it, *en rapport* with it. And he thought that being *en rapport* involved three things: One must possess a name for the entity that (1) denoted the entity, (2) is for the user a "vivid" name and (3) in a technical sense, is a name for the speaker for the object. For the latter condition to be satisfied the entity must enter into the "genetic" account of how the speaker came to acquire the name, the beliefs that he would express using the name, etc. I do not believe that he succeeds in spelling out exactly how the entity must enter into the account any more than have others who have suggested some similar condition, but he has a nice analogy with the notion of when a picture is a picture of something (as opposed to merely resembling something) where it seems clear that a similar genetic requirement operates. Now for my own part I am inclined to drop Kaplan's first two requirements and try to go with some variant of this third condition as being what is required for a name to be a name that a speaker can use to assert *de re* something *about* an entity. I am, of course, not going to attempt any defense of that sort of claim here, but if it were correct it would, of course, account for why the sort of stipulations we have been discussing do not put us in a position to assert and, thus, to know anything about the entity for which we have introduced a rigid designator.

One final remark: Having indicated the direction in which I am inclined to go, I find myself wanting to ask the question, why, if indeed it is true, is one in a position to assert and know *de re* things about an entity when the entity becomes (in the right way) a part of the history of one's use of the name? What does *that* accomplish that allows for this possibility? But perhaps that is a misconceived question. Perhaps the only answer is that that is just when we do ascribe *de re* propositional attitudes. Perhaps the only task we can perform is the one Kaplan was attempting, to make sure that we have spelled out as exactly as possible the conditions under which such attitudes are correctly ascribed.

NOTES

1. In *Semantics of Natural Language*, ed. D. Davidson and G. Harman (Dordrecht, 1972), pp. 253–355.
2. *Ibid.*, p. 269. Strictly we should add, as Kripke points out, "if the term designates anything in that possible world."
3. *Ibid.*, p. 263.
4. *Ibid.*, pp. 347–8, n. 33.
5. (New York, 1973), pp. 110–151.
6. "Naming and Necessity," p. 348, n. 33.
7. I modify Kripke's description of the case to provide a "definite" definite description to work with.
8. On the other hand it must be admitted that we have possessed various natural ways of expressing the intention to introduce a term as an abbreviation for an expression.
9. "Proper Names and Identifying Descriptions," *Synthese* 21 (1970): 335–358, reprinted in *Semantics of Natural Language*, ed. D. Davidson and G. Harman, pp. 356–379.
10. Suppose, however, that someone were to hold the following sort of view about the status of a name such as "Aristotle": At some point there was an original dubbing of a person giving him that name. The name is passed along to others not present at the dubbing. At least in many cases this is accomplished by one person deciding to use the name to refer to what another who already possesses the use of the name refers to. And such a person is to be considered as introducing the name into his own repertoire as a rigid designator using some such description as "the individual to whom Jones was referring when he used the name 'Aristotle' " to fix the reference. I believe it would be a consequence of the position of this paper that the person would not thereby be put in a position to *use* the name. And that would seem to show that sort of view of how names are passed along wrong.
11. "Speaking of Nothing," *Philosophical Review*, 83 (1974): 3–31.
12. "Quantifying In," *Words and Objections, Essays on the Work of W. V. Quine*, ed. D. Davidson and J. Hintikka (Dordrecht, 1969), pp. 206–242. In this paper, however, Kaplan adds two other relations so that his view is not a pure example of the kind of view I have in mind.
13. *Frege*, p. 121.
14. The conclusion that this is the correct characterization of the matter is not original to this paper. It is suggested by at least two authors that I know of, Alvin Plantinga [*The Nature of Necessity*, (Oxford, 1974), pp. 8–9, n. 1] and Michael Levin ["Kripke's Argument Against the Identity Thesis," *The Journal of Philosophy* 72 (1975), 152, n. 21. My excuse for a longer discussion is the need for a fuller exposition and an investigation of the consequences.
15. "The Causal Theory of Names," *Proceedings of the Aristotelian Society*, Suppl. Vol. 47 (1973): 192.

16. "Modality, De Dicto and De Re," in *Logic, Methodology and the Philosophy of Science: Proceedings of the 1960 International Congress* (Stanford, 1962), pp. 629–30. Kripke's discussion occurs on pages 283–4 of "Naming and Necessity." Kripke's "quark" example (p. 284) could be used to make the same point using a common noun instead of a name.
17. I utilize a stipulation about the contingent truth of a certain sentence for heuristic purposes—I do not believe it plays an essential role in my argument. There may be some difficulties involved with this sort of stipulation. One possible objection to the device in the simple form I give it in the text (suggested to me in correspondence by Plantinga) is that anyone who thought names to be disguised descriptions might hold that the device would succeed only in introducing "N" as an abbreviation for a certain description. The only plausible candidates, however, for what that definite description would be seem to be either "the ϕ" or "the thing denoted by 'the ϕ.'" "The thing denoted by 'the ϕ' is the ϕ" and "the ϕ is the ϕ" are, it could be argued, only contingently true when true because they express something false of worlds in which the ϕ does not exist. We could avoid this objection, I believe, in one of two ways. We could define a notion of "strictly contingent" according to which a sentence expresses a strictly contingent truth only if the sentence would express a falsehood in some worlds in which there is a denotation for any definite descriptions contained in the sentence. Or we could change the form or the stipulation to read: "Provided the ϕ exists, let 'If the ϕ exists, N is the ϕ' express a contingent truth." (I suppose there would also have to be some other conditions understood—for example, that the words in the quoted sentence, other than the introduced name, have their usual meanings and references.)
18. "Naming and Necessity," pp. 346–7, n. 26. emphasis his.
19. This volume, pp. 383–400.
20. If some of Kripke's other views are correct, I believe there will be definite descriptions that denote things other than abstract formal objects that will also turn out to be rigid designators. He holds, for example, that certain identity statements concerning natural kinds are, if true, necessarily true, though discoverable as true only *a posteriori*. One such statement he mentions is the statement that gold is the element with atomic number 79. This would entail that the definite description, "the element with atomic number 79" is a rigid designator, designating the same thing, i.e. same substance, in all possible worlds, namely, providing the statement in question is true, gold. Now I know that the element with atomic number 79 has more than seventy-eight protons in its atomic nucleus, but since I have not checked to make sure Kripke made no mistake in his example, I would not claim to know this about gold.
21. The problems have been posed forcefully by Diana Ackerman in comments in a symposium at the 1974 Eastern Division A.P.A. meetings and in an unpublished paper, "Proper Names and Propositional Attitudes."

22. I have in mind the "Hesperus" and "Phosphorus" kind of cases. According to the usual story the ancient Babylonians used these as names for what they took to be two distinct heavenly bodies but which was in fact one, Venus. They believed—in fact, I think we can say, knew—that Hesperus was the first heavenly body to appear in the evening, but they would have denied that they believed this of Phosphorus. Did they nevertheless know this about Phosphorus, which, after all, is Hesperus? And should we say about them that they knew about Venus, though they did not call it by that name, that it was the first to appear in the evening? The structure of this sort of case that gives rise to the problems does not seem to me to be present in the "Neptune" and "Newman 1" examples and so there seems no reason why the "loose" principles that I give should not apply to them if they do in fact present examples of knowledge. Also, I *do* have some temptation, at any rate, to say of the Babylonians that they knew about Venus, etc., but I have no corresponding temptation in the "Neptune" and "Newman 1" examples.
23. "Quantifying In," pp. 228–29.
24. This was suggested in discussion by Rogers Albritton.

[7]

KRIPKE AND PUTNAM ON NATURAL KIND TERMS*

The theory of natural kinds terms developed by Saul Kripke and Hilary Putnam is seen by both authors, I believe, as being intimately connected to Kripke's views about reference, perhaps even a consequence of them.[1] The views about reference, however, were first applied to singular terms and one wonders whether the transition to a theory about general terms, terms for kinds of things, can be made without more complications than either author, in my opinion, clearly indicates.

I want to examine, then, the application of some of the central ideas Kripke developed concerning singular terms to general terms for kinds. In particular, I will be concerned with his notion of rigid designation and the generation of, what I call, "exotic" necessary truths. I will try to show that the theory of natural kind terms must in fact use additional ideas and different argumentation. In doing this I will not, generally, be uncovering things only implicit in the writings of Kripke and Putnam; for the most part they are there to be seen. But I think it is easy to be misled about what is going on and, I think, the authors themselves sometimes go wrong

First published in *Knowledge and Mind: Philosophical Essays*, C. Ginet and S. Shoemaker, eds., New York: Oxford University Press, 1983, pp. 84–104.

in describing their own procedures. My own feeling is that when one sees more clearly what is involved some interesting puzzles emerge. At the end I try to develop an outline of one of these.

I

Before getting down to details it would be useful to look at some general features of the Kripke-Putnam treatment of natural kind terms. In the first place most of the examples they use are words and expressions in everyday use, such as 'water,' 'tiger,' 'gold,' and 'heat.' While the theory calls for a certain relationship between the semantics of these terms and science, the terms obviously are not borrowed from the vocabulary of science and were part of English long before the advent of modern science. I think it is no accident that terms with these characteristics were chosen. In the first place, although one might suppose that if terms for natural kinds are to be found anywhere the language of science would be replete with them, it is not obvious that the Kripke-Putnam theory is applicable to kind terms in science. Nor is it obvious that it will apply to terms which the vernacular has borrowed from the language of science, such as 'plutonium' or 'electron.'

Putting aside, however, the doubts just expressed, there is a second reason for choosing as examples terms from the vernacular that antedate the rise of science: The Kripke-Putnam theory offers an answer to an important puzzle about the relationship of vernacular kind terms and scientific discovery. We seem willing to tailor the application of many of our vernacular terms for kinds to the results of science and if necessary to allow our usual means of determining the extension of these terms to be overridden. There is, for example, a product on the market composed half of sodium chloride and half of potassium chloride. It looks like and tastes like ordinary salt. In most ordinary circumstances—in talking about how much to put in the stew, for example—we would be happy to call this product "salt" even if we knew its chemical composition. But if pressed to say whether this product is "really" salt, I think we would, if we know some elementary chemistry and the chemical composition of the product, concede that it is only half salt. To take a couple of more examples, I would give up calling a stone purchased as a diamond a 'diamond' if assured by experts that it did not possess a certain crystalline structure of carbon and I am prepared to be corrected when what I take to be a wolf in a cage at the zoo turns out to be identified by zoologists as being of a quite distinct species.

This apparent reliance on results and classification raises a question about the extension and meaning of kind terms in the vernacular prior to investigation. It is at least plausible that prior to modern chemistry, crystallography, and zoology a mixture of sodium and potassium chlorides, a sparkling clear crystal of some other substance than carbon, and an animal looking exactly like a wolf, but of that other species, might be called 'salt,' 'a diamond,' and 'a wolf' without a way for anyone to be the wiser.

Several questions come up at this point. Is the extension of the terms in question as used prior to the relevant results the same as or different from the extension of the terms as used today? Is the meaning of the terms the same or different? And what is the status of the results? To take the term 'salt' as an instance, it seems very plausible to say that at a certain point it was experimentally discovered that salt is the compound sodium chloride. Subsequently, knowledgeable speakers appear to use the property of being sodium chloride as the ultimate criterion for whether or not a bit of stuff is "really" salt. One common response to these observations is that prior to the scientific discovery being sodium chloride was not a part of what it meant to be salt, but that after the scientific discovery (for whatever reason), it became a part of (perhaps the whole of) the meaning of the term 'salt.' This, however, has some unintuitive consequences. First, it implies that in this instance as in many others a word has changed its meaning due to a scientific discovery. But we do not generally suppose that when we see a word such as 'salt' in, say, John Locke's *Essay Concerning the Human Understanding*, it has a different meaning. There is also the not unlikely possibility that if such a view of the situation is correct then the extension of such a term has also changed. And, finally, it is difficult to see how we can *now* speak of an experimental result if we have made it part of the very meaning of 'salt' that salt is sodium chloride.

The Kripke-Putnam view seems to have the virtue that none of these unintuitive results need be accepted. The facts as presented do not show, on their view, that, e.g., the word 'salt' has changed its meaning from, say, Locke's day to ours or that it has changed its extension. People in Locke's day might have called some stuff 'salt' that we would not (on the grounds that the stuff is not sodium chloride) but that does not show that the extension is different, only that (providing that our chemists have got things correct) people in Locke's day made mistakes which they had no means to correct. And finally that salt is sodium chloride was and remains a statement of an experimental discovery.

II

The way in which the results mentioned in the last section may seem to come about is through the application to kind terms of a now well-known, but still startling, result that Kripke obtained for proper names. Proper names, according to Kripke (and I agree with this) are what he calls "rigid designators." It will suffice for our purposes to characterize a rigid designator as a term which designates the same individual in all possible worlds. It will be recalled that in both "Naming and Necessity" and in "Identity and Necessity" Kripke introduces the notion first in connection with what are loosely called "singular terms." In particular, proper names are, in general, rigid while definite descriptions, for the most part, are not.

It will be recalled that one of the startling results Kripke obtains is that in regard to terms rigidly designating *contingently* existing objects (as opposed, say, to mathematical objects), certain sentences involving such terms turn out to express necessary truths, although the fact that they express truths is to be learned by empirical means. I have called such truths "exotic necessary truths."[2]

I suppose one reason that this result is startling, aside from the fact that it represents a possibility not countenanced in philosophy before, is that since necessary truths are true in all possible worlds they do not distinguish the actual world from other possible worlds and so it looks as if an examination of how the actual world *is* could have no bearing on establishing the truth.

In any event, providing we accept the notion, rigid designators for individuate produce exotic necessary truths in a relatively simple manner. I stress this because I think matters to be different when we turn to terms for kinds.

Restricting ourselves to contingently existing individuate, exotic necessary truths arise when there are two rigid designators for the same individual. Kripke's main examples are sentences expressing the relation of identity in which, to put it loosely, the identity sign is flanked by two different rigid designators, designating the same individual. So if 'D' and 'D′' are two such terms the sentence

D is identical with D′

expresses an exotic necessary truth. And the argument is simply this: since by hypothesis 'D' and also 'D′' designate the same individual in all possible worlds they must designate that individual in each case. But since, by hypothesis, they designate the same individual in this world they must do so in all possible worlds. Hence, the sentence expresses a necessary truth. The sentence expresses an exotic necessary truth for the following reason: While it may be possible for someone not to have to do any research about the actual world in order to know that such a sentence expresses a truth—as when, for example, one is introduced to a person and in the same breath given two names for him—it is obviously possible, and does occur, that a person or a culture has two names for the same individual without realizing it. So we have the stock examples of someone having both the names 'Cicero' and 'Tully' without realizing that, as they are used by him, they name one and the same person, and (what historically seems to me questionable) the story of the Babylonians having given the names 'Hesperus' and 'Phosphorus' to the planet Venus without realizing that a single heavenly body had been named. Under these circumstances, empirical investigation is required to ascertain that the identity sentence in question expresses a truth.

If this short exposition of Kripke's view about proper names is correct, it generates "exotic necessary truths" using essentially just the notions of rigid designation and identity.

What I want to argue is that this is not enough to give us the theory of natural kind terms that Kripke and Putnam want. Rigid designation (and identity), which gives the spectacular results for proper names, is not enough to do the same thing in the case of general terms for kinds. I do not mean to say that Kripke and Putnam would disagree with this, but Putnam says, for example, in his treatment of the term 'water,' "Our discussion leans heavily on the work of Saul Kripke although conclusions were obtained independently" and then "... we may express Kripke's theory and mine by saying, for example, that the term 'water' is rigid."[3]

My view is that here Putnam is wrong about the mechanism of his own view. However, I also find in some of Kripke's descriptions of *his* argument the same mistake. Kripke does use an argument in the earlier version of his view, "Identity and Necessity," which does seem to extend in a simple manner the results and argumentation from proper names to (natural) kind terms. The problem is that it will not work.

But Putnam and Kripke (in the later work, "Naming and Necessity") use, on my reading, a more complicated argument. I want to question the latter argument as well, but to do so requires considerations which are more difficult to assess.

I want to argue that one cannot transfer, in a straightforward way, the Kripke results about proper names to terms for kinds, even though in the next section I assume that Kripke and Putnam must treat kind terms as being singular terms.

III

In trying to extend the notion of a rigid designator to non-singular terms we immediately come up against a problem which, I believe, neither Kripke nor Putnam touch upon. Rigid designation was initially defined by Kripke for singular terms—those terms which in some way carry along with them the requirement that there is a single individual referred to. A term such as 'tiger,' unless it occurs in some such context as 'The tiger who bit my friend,' does not at first glance seem to refer to any individual. Philosophers talk about the *extension* of a term and usually apply this notion both to singular terms, such as names, and general terms such as 'tiger.' The extension of a term is, roughly, what it applies to correctly.

Now if by talking about what is designated by a term in all possible worlds we were to think of the *extension* of the term 'tiger' we would not find it to be a rigid designator. In different possible worlds there are more or fewer tigers than in this and I suppose that the particular tigers of the actual world do not exist in all possible worlds.

For the purposes of this paper I am going to assume that construing terms for kinds, such as 'water,' 'tiger,' etc., as rigid designators *and* giving the Kripke-Putnam view the best run for its money is to think of them as what Mill calls "abstract" nouns. 'Tiger' is not to be thought of as designating its extension. Rather, it designates (is the name of) a certain species. 'Water' designates, not *its* extension—puddles, pools, ponds of stuff—but the substance, water. Thought of in this way, kind terms are in one way like proper names: they designate a single entity, albeit an abstract entity—a species or a substance in these cases. I am aware that there are other suggestions about how to construe kind terms for the Kripke-Putnam theory. I don't believe that any are better suited, but the issue needs to be argued. All I will say here is that I think I can show that no other way has fewer problems for their view.[4]

If I am correct, a problem now arises. One would suppose that there is going to come out of the Kripke-Putnam view a distinction between general terms which designate natural kinds and general terms which do not. And there is at least the suggestion that rigid designation is the key. But, taken as "abstract" nouns, terms that seem intuitively to be obvious examples of non-natural kind terms seem just as rigid as those Kripke and Putnam use as examples of natural kind terms. Taken as abstract nouns there seems to be no difference at all between terms we would naturally suppose to fall in one class and terms we would naturally suppose to fall into the other in respect to rigidity. This was noted by David Kaplan in a footnote to his paper "Bob and Carol and Ted and Alice."[5]

One would naturally suppose that some such term as 'bachelorhood' would fall on the side of non-natural kind terms. But as an "abstract" noun it seems to be just as much a rigid designator as 'tiger' or 'water.' Rigid designation seems to provide no difference between natural and non-natural kind terms.

IV

Now, I want to identify the argument about "natural kind terms" which seems to me to be the straightforward extension of what Kripke shows about proper names and which seems to me not to work for general terms. I quote from a passage in Kripke's "Identity and Necessity" in which he seems to argue merely from the rigidity of the abstract nouns (or, to be accurate, nouns and noun phrases) that a certain statement is an exotic necessary truth. Kripke has just been discussing the statement that heat is the motion of molecules. He says,

> To state the view succinctly: we use both the terms 'heat' and 'the motion of molecules' as rigid designators for a certain external phenomenon. Since heat is in fact the motion of molecules, and the designators are rigid, by the argument I have given here, it is going to be *necessary* that heat is the motion o£molecules.[6]

Some comments on this passage: First, Kripke takes the terms 'heat' and 'the motion of molecules' as functioning in the sentence 'Heat is the motion of molecules' as what I have called an abstract noun (or an abstract noun phrase). Second, he is treating the statement in question as an *identity* statement. Third, when he says "by the argument I have given here" I take him to mean the general argument of the paper as applied to this example. And the general argument started out with a consideration of proper names and includes the following passage:

> If names are rigid designators, then there can be no question about identities being necessary, because '*a*' and '*V*' will be rigid designators of a certain man or thing *x*. Then even in every possible world, *a* and *b* [*sic*] will both refer to this same object *x*, and to no other, and so there will be no situation in which *a* might not have been *b*.[7]

So the argument seems to be the same one given in the case of proper names and to depend simply on the rigidity of the terms involved. And this may seem to go against my saying that it won't do to sum up the view about natural kind terms by saying that such-and-such a natural kind term is a rigid designator. For if the argument about proper names is sound, this one seems sound also. But there are problems. For example: I would suppose that both Putnam and Kripke would consider it likely that the following statements are, if true, necessarily true:

(a) Tigers are mammals.
(b) Water is a compound, not an element.

Neither of these, obviously, is an identity statement. So even given that the terms 'mammal' and 'a compound not an element' are rigid designators of certain kinds, the simple argument which can be applied to names cannot be used. Of course, if we already knew the truth of some identity statement from which (a) or (b) followed, and if the identity statement were an exotic necessary truth, then a simple extension of the argument would give the desired result. For instance, if we know that *heat is the motion of molecules* is an exotic necessary truth then we can simply deduce that heat is some state or other of molecules—the latter not being an identity statement.

But we need not know any such identity statement in order to discover (and historically I would guess this is the actual situation) that (a) or (b) is true. I am not even sure that in the case of (a), at least, we even now have any *identity* statement from which it can be deduced that tigers are mammals.

It might be said that all I have shown is that we can know that (a) and (b) are true without being in a position to know that they are exotic necessary truths: that to know the latter we would have to await the discovery of some exotic necessarily true identity statement. My point, however, will be that on the more complex theory, as I understand it, we *could* know that (a) and (b) are exotic necessary truths without awaiting the appearance of some identity statement which we can know to have that property. And this is another reason why we should not sum up Kripke's or Putnam's view by saying that this or that term is a rigid designator.

V

Now I want to imagine time-transporting John Locke to our era and convincing him of our scientific results and also teaching him what is meant by a rigid designator. I choose to transport *Locke* because I think his view about terms for natural kinds (he uses the expression "names of substances," but the topic is the same) represents an enemy for Kripke and Putnam. Locke, on my reading, is willing to allow that there might be something like natural *kinds* (divisions in nature as a consequence of the primary qualities of what we might now think of as such things as atoms, molecules, genes, etc.), but that we don't have terms in the vernacular the extensions of which are determined by such divisions in nature. Instead, he believed that while men are inclined to believe that many of their kind terms are dependent upon nature in some such way, in fact the extensions of our vernacular kind terms are determined by the properties each of us uses to decide on the application of them. (To use Putnam's apt phrase, Locke holds that the meaning of kind terms are in "the head.") One might say that he held that while there may be natural *kinds*, there are no natural kind *terms*, at least in the vernacular.

But Locke transported here and now, given current philosophic and scientific theories, could, I believe, agree with both and still maintain his position. He could, that is, if the philosophic training only utilizes the argument based on rigid designation and identity that I find in the passages quoted from Kripke's earlier paper—the argument which seems to be the simple application of the ideas developed for proper names.

Using Kripke's example, he could admit that 'heat' and 'the motion of molecules' used as abstract noun and noun phrase are rigid designators and, given that he believes our science (or what we are pretending here is our science), that the extensions of these terms are the same. But he could not hold that any discovery shows that the identity statement expressed by the sentence using these terms as *abstract nouns* is true.

Given that he would suppose, as I think he would, that we have different necessary and sufficient criteria for the correct application of the terms 'heat' and 'the motion of molecules' in our minds, there is no way for science to discover that these *kinds* of phenomena are identical; in fact, there is no way in which the *kinds* could be identical. The situation for Locke would be the same as it is in fact for the terms 'hearted thing' and 'livered thing'—as abstract noun phrases they designate different kinds, although their extensions are, in the actual world, identical.

What Locke easily concedes is that each kind term (or expression) names the very same *kind* in all possible worlds and so is a rigid designator. What he would deny is that we have discovered an *identity* between *kinds*. Perhaps we have discovered a *co-extension* in the actual world, but that won't produce the desired result.

The reason why the argument we have looked at, using rigid designation and identity alone, works with proper names and not with kind terms is, of course, that proper names are singular and kind terms are general terms. If two *singular* terms are both rigid designators and their extension is the same, then there is just one individual that both terms designate in this, the actual, world and the same individual must be so designated in all possible worlds.

But, if we are dealing with two *kind* terms, their extensions might be the same in this, the actual, world without it being true that the two terms are names of *identical kinds*. What Locke might say, then, at this point is that co-extension of instances of two *kind* terms, even though each is a rigid designator as the name of a kind, doesn't show at all that the two *kinds* are identical.

VI

To obtain the same results for kind terms as Kripke obtained for proper names—especially the generation of "exotic" necessary truths—we need something more. And both Kripke and Putnam, as I read them, try to do this. I am going to use Putnam, but Kripke has the same augmented apparatus. Here are two connected quotes from Putnam about 'water':

> To be water, for example, is to bear the relation same_L [same liquid] to certain things.[8]

And

> x bears the relation same_L to y just in case (i) x and y are both liquids, and (2) x and y agree in important physical properties.[9]

These are two passages from the same paper in which Putnam says that his view and Kripke's can be summed up by saying that, e.g., 'water' is a rigid designator. But what new material is introduced in these representative passages! Nothing about "important physical properties" is needed or used in Kripke's arguments about proper names to generate exotic necessary truths. Here then is the something more.

As a first shot I believe we can capture the idea in the following principle:

> (P) Something is water just in case it is a liquid and agrees in its important physical properties with the general run of stuff which English speakers call 'water.'

(That the term 'water' is mentioned does not, I believe, lead to difficulties as it would were we giving a classical definition.) The use of "the general run of stuff which English speakers call 'water' " can be explicated as follows: A word such as 'water' comes into a language as a word for a certain kind of stuff and ordinary users of the word will usually be able to apply the word by having learned to recognize certain characteristic "surface" properties—roughly those one can discern by relatively unsophisticated uses of the senses.

One complication I will ignore is that even before scientists, who are supposed to uncover the important physical properties, come into the picture there may be room for what Putnam calls a "division of linguistic labor" which is not reflected in (P). There may be users of the language who, although they have a term in their vocabulary and even may be said to "know the meaning," do not have a sufficient grasp of what surface properties to look for to be able to recognize instances of what the term is supposed to apply to. I think that this is probably what Putnam's situation is concerning the terms 'elm' and 'beech,' a situation which I share with him. I cannot tell the difference between these two trees, but what I need—at least for such purposes as ordering from a tree farm—is not a scientist, but more likely a knowledgeable gardener. Since it would be absurd for anyone who wants to investigate the important physical properties of elms or beeches to consult me, even though I am an English-speaking user of the terms in question, a modification of (P) may be in order. But, as I say, I think we can ignore this here.

It does, however, seem in order to modify (P) so as to reflect the important fact that Putnam wants his mechanism to function across possible worlds. To capture this, let us modify (P) to get:

> (P′) For all worlds W, something is water in W just in case it is a liquid and agrees in its important physical properties with the general run of stuff which English speakers call 'water' in the actual world.

It follows from (P′) that the extension of the term 'water' in any possible world is not determined by the surface properties which ordinary people may use to decide whether or not some bit of stuff is water, but rather by the important physical properties. And these, presumably, fall within the province of scientists. Now if being H_2O

is one of the important physical properties of the general run of stuff English speakers call 'water,' then that water is H_2O is what I have called an exotic necessary truth. Its truth is a discovery of science and by P′ it is true in all possible worlds. But notice that this result is not a consequence simply of the fact that the term 'water,' taken as an abstract noun, is a rigid designator, but rather from the more complicated features of (P′), in particular its use of the notion of *important physical properties* of samples of stuff in the actual world.

There may seem to be another interesting and important consequence of Putnam's mechanism. Since it is the important physical properties, properties to be discovered by what probably has to be a sophisticated science, and not the surface properties, which determine the extension of a term such as 'water,' it may seem to follow that prior to the rise of such a science users of the term, relying solely on surface properties, can be wrong—at least in some cases—when even after a most careful examination they call some bit of stuff 'water.' For it may not be H_2O. This is a result Putnam in fact insists upon, and one I wish to raise a question about.

VII

In his article, "The Meaning of 'Meaning,'" Putnam makes use of an ingenious set of "Twin-Earth" examples. I want to do something similar. I want to imagine two cultures which up to a certain point in their history are as alike as one can make them. In particular, the languages they speak are identical, or, at any rate, there is nothing up to the date mentioned which affords a basis for positing a difference. I want also to imagine that at a certain period in their histories each culture develops a sophisticated science and view of the world and that these also are identical down to the smallest detail.

Now let us take one of the terms for kinds which existed in the vernacular languages prior to the rise of science. I want to argue that although that term, by hypothesis, would exhibit no linguistic differences in the two languages prior to the rise of science, and although the sciences developed are identical, the term could come to have a different extension in each culture. Or, to be more accurate, I want to argue that Putnam's account of natural kind terms allows for this result.

It will be somewhat simpler for my purposes if I temporarily shift examples—changing water into gold. One of Kripke's examples of what I have been calling exotic necessary truths is the statement that gold has atomic number 79. I feel sure that Putnam would regard atomic number—the number of protons in the nucleus of the atom of an element—as an important physical property.

If I understand Putnam's mechanism correctly, he would also agree that John Locke might have been mistaken, say, about the composition of a ring he valued for its gold content if, in fact, the material it was made of did not consist mainly of atoms having atomic number 79, even if the foremost goldsmith of his day would have, on the basis of careful scrutiny of its surface properties, said it was undoubtedly gold.

For convenience we may as well imagine that my two cultures exist on Earth and Twin-Earth, much as in Putnam's examples. I will imagine then that my Twin-Earth has the same history as Earth up to some point in the earlier part of their twentieth century. In particular there has been a group of people, including the doppelganger of John Locke, speaking a language called by them 'English' indistinguishable in every respect to an outside observer from the language of the same name spoken on Earth. At some point early in the twentieth century they developed an atomic theory, once more indistinguishable from that developed on Earth. In particular they see the atom as having a nucleus composed of positively charged particles, which they call 'protons,' and neutrally charged particles, which they call 'neutrons.' In their laboratories their scientists speak of 'elements' and use this term in the same way that our scientists have, for those non-compound substances whose atoms have a particular number of protons in the nucleus—what they and we call the 'atomic number.' They also recognize, and use the word, 'isotopes,' isotopes being individuated by the combined number of protons and neutrons in the nucleus of the atom—that number being the isotope number.[10] They also have, as our scientists have, come to realize that the same element may have, and usually will have, several different isotopes and they give them names for use in the laboratory as our scientists have given the names 'protium,' 'deuterium,' and 'tritium' to the three known isotopes of what *we* call 'hydrogen.' These similarities are all that I really need for the point I wish to make, so for the rest of the two developments in science, imagine that Twin-Earth and Earth are identical. I have thus, I believe, so built my story that the scientific picture of the world is the same in the first parts of the twentieth century for both cultures.

Although I believe that what I will now imagine is not strictly speaking necessary for what I will propose, it may help to make the situation psychologically more plausible. I imagine then that on Twin-Earth not only do elements usually have several isotopes, but also it is a general rule that one of the isotopes of a particular element makes up the bulk of the element as it occurs in nature—the other isotopes being fairly rare. I do not off-hand know whether this situation in fact obtains on Earth. If it does then I have made no change as yet between Earth and Twin-Earth. But even if it does not, the change I will have made is simply one concerning the relative distribution of things and will have nothing to do with a difference in scientific outlook, any more than the fact that we have less and less oil changes our scientific theories.

Now what isotope one is dealing with makes a big difference in how one will expect some bit of matter to behave. Just to mention a couple of the few things that I know about it, it is often the case that some isotopes of an element are radioactive and others not, and this, of course, has had profound consequences. Also some isotopes of the same element are unstable and break down into an isotope of another element. I believe this is the basis of carbon 14 dating. Of course, what element is in question is also of very great importance, especially in chemical reactions. But it might be a close question as to whether isotope number or atomic number has more importance.

Now with these suppositions and facts, it seems to me not psychologically implausible for my Twin-Earthlings to be more taken with, so to speak, the isotope number of a bit of substance rather than with its atomic number and also not implausible for them to diverge from our practice and to identify the substance designated by some of their vernacular natural kind terms not with a certain element, but with the isotope which makes up the bulk of what had been previously called by that term. Hence, for example, they identify gold, not with the element having atomic number 79, but with a certain isotope having a certain isotope number. The rare isotopes of the element having number 79 would then be dismissed as not "really" being gold, although, to be sure, in various ways very much like gold.

If I have described a possible Twin-Earth situation, then were my doppelganger on Twin-Earth to ask someone in the Twin-Earth UCLA chemistry department what gold is, he would be told that it is a substance having such-and-such isotope number, while I, in the analogous situation, would be told that it is a substance having atomic number so-and-so. It should be obvious that if I and my doppelganger defer to scientists as Putnam supposes we would, the extension of his term 'gold' and of mine will at this point diverge.

My story can, obviously, be extended to the vernacular term 'water.' On Twin-Earth, in my story, because isotopes are taken more seriously for one or another practical or historical reason, we can suppose that Twin-Earthlings will identify water with protium oxide and exclude what we call 'heavy water'—deuterium or tritium oxide.

After the scientific discoveries and the mapping of non-scientific kind terms onto them, there will be a difference between Twin-Earthlings and Earthlings in regard to the truth-value of what certain sentences express. For example, there will be a sentence of the form 'Some gold has isotope number x and some gold has isotope number y' which Earthlings will take to express a truth and Twin-Earthlings a falsehood. Correspondingly, while the sentence 'Gold has atomic number 79' will be regarded as expressing a truth by Twin-Earthlings provided 'has' does not carry with it the notion of identity, 'Gold is *identical* with the element having atomic number 79' will be regarded by them as expressing something false, while Earthlings will regard it as expressing something true.

We cannot immediately conclude that in my story it turns out that Twin-Earthlings regard certain *propositions* as true which Earthlings regard as false and *vice versa,* for it is open to one to say that the corresponding sentences do not express the same thing. In fact, in my story it would be paradoxical to conclude that the two parties have different beliefs about what is true or false because that would imply that there is a right and a wrong in the matter. And there does not seem to be any way of showing that either party is right while the other is wrong.

My talk about "mapping" ordinary language terms onto science may suggest a historical two-stage process: first there is science and its divisions of things into kinds, and then there is the hookup of natural language terms—with some leeway in theory, if not in psychological reality, about how this second stage is carried out. I do not believe I need suppose this to be possible. Perhaps science has to begin with questions about kinds of things couched in ordinary language: "What is the nature of gold?," "What is the nature of water?," etc. Even if that is so, Twin-Earthlings in my story come up with verbally different things from Earthlings even though they start from what is to all appearances the same language and even though their science turns out to be identical. (Even if science must begin from questions couched in ordinary language, it soon develops its own terms for natural kinds: The names of elements low on the periodic chart, in our science, are taken from ordinary language; those discovered later have invented names, and there are vastly more invented names for compounds than ones derived from ordinary language.)

What do I conclude from my story? I do not draw the conclusion that Putnam has failed to describe how natural kind terms in the vernacular function. The story does not show that. But I do think that two important points emerge. First, there is a certain slackness in the machinery which Putnam does not, I feel, prepare us for. In my story science develops apart on Earth and Twin-Earth. The slackness comes from how ordinary language terms for *kinds* are mapped onto the same classifications. In my story I have envisaged only a small wobble; how much latitude there might be in theory I do not know. The point is that we can agree with Putnam's theory about how natural kinds terms function in ordinary language and still see that we might have done things differently even with the very same results.

The second consequence flows out of the first. Putnam's view, it will be recalled, is that the extension of a term such as 'gold' or 'water' would be the same before discoveries about important physical properties as it was afterward. John Locke would have been wrong, however justified he might have been, had he thought something to be gold or water which did not have the important physical properties discovered later. My strong inclination is to agree with Putnam that when I see the words 'gold' and 'water' in Locke's *Essay on the Human Understanding* there is no "change of meaning." And I also am strongly inclined to agree that I would not count something as, strictly speaking, *water* unless it were H_2O, or as *gold* unless it had the atomic number our scientists say that gold has. But I am an Earthling. In my story Twin-Earthlings do things slightly differently, although for no reasons having to do with a different linguistic basis or a different science. What should we then say about the extension of such ordinary language terms for kinds?

If you accept that my story of Earth and Twin-Earth contains no inconsistencies or other mistakes, then I do not see how we can accept Putnam's view that it is clear that natural kind terms in ordinary language have the same extension before and after scientific discoveries and the mapping of those terms on to those discoveries. The "slackness" I have talked about seems to allow that from the very same linguistic base we may, after the very same scientific discoveries, move in different directions. Which way we move will change the extension. How can we then say that, given that we have moved in one direction, the users of the ordinary language terms might just have been dead wrong in applying the term to some particular instance? Locke's ring, which he took to be gold, might have been made of stuff having atomic number 79. In my story, the Earthling Putnam would say that Locke was correct. But suppose his ring were made of one of the rare isotopes, as we would say, of gold. Twin-Earthlings would say the ring wasn't made of gold at all. Putnam's doppelganger would conclude that Locke was dead wrong. But nothing about language or science explains this difference.

You might object at this point that I have not kept my Twin-Earthlings as much the same as us as I have made it seem. After all, they do take a different turn; and must this not mean that they had at least one psychological difference from us?—they had the disposition to be struck more by isotopes than by elements. And perhaps this disposition in some way ought to count as showing a difference in the language, however much it looked to be the same as ours prior to scientific discoveries. Even if we admit that there was at some point a disposition on their part which we do not have, the disposition may not always have been there. We need not suppose that because the twentieth-century Twin-Earthlings had this disposition, the eighteenth-century ones did also. Nor do we need to suppose that there was such a disposition even in twentieth-century Twin-Earthlings prior to their looking at their scientific theory. Thus we seem to have no reason to think that their John Locke and ours differed psychologically or linguistically. Or rather we have none unless we accept what seems to be an outrageously bizarre view of language—that the extension of one's terms may be determined by the psychological quirks of some people several centuries hence.

There is one point about the scientific situation in regard to atomic theory that I have left out of my story. Historically, the discovery of the possibility of isotopes, and of the big difference it makes which one is involved, carne after the development of the simpler atomic theory which included the notion of elements and atomic numbers. Possibly this historical accident had an influence on the way in which we mapped our vernacular natural kind terms onto science. But this would be of little comfort to Putnam, I should think. It seems just as bizarre to suppose that the extension of one's terms should depend upon such future historical accidents as it does to suppose that they depend upon future psychological quirks.

To sum up then, if we go along with Putnam a certain distance we seem either to have to embrace unacceptable views about language or to admit that nature, after all, does not fully determine the extension of vernacular natural kind terms, and science is not wholly responsible for discovering their true extensions.

NOTES

* Norman Malcolm has been a great influence on my philosophical thinking and remains so. I wish that my contribution to this volume in his honor were on a topic for which he is well known. A seminar on dreaming which I gave last year did not result in anything which I considered an original contribution on my part. Hence, this contribution of mine simply represents my own current philosophical interest. It benefits from discussion with, among others, Jay Atlas, Tyler Burge, David Kaplan, and Jon Wilwerding. The latter has independently developed an example somewhat like the one given by me in the last section, but from which he has been able to derive somewhat stronger conclusions than I do here.

1. For Kripke's views I use "Identity and Necessity" in M. K. Munitz, ed., *Identity and Individuation* (New York: New York University Press, 1971), pp. 135–64; and "Naming and Necessity" in Davidson and Harman, eds., *Semantics of Natural Language* (Dordrecht: D. Reidel, 1972), pp. 253–354. For Putnam's views I use "The Meaning of 'Meaning'" in his *Mina, Language and Reality* (Cambridge: Cambridge University Press, 1975), vol. 2, pp. 215–17.
2. I introduce the expression "exotic necessary truths" not just to dramatize the interest of Kripke's discovery. The more obvious term "*a posteriori* truths" obscures an important point. If we distinguish a sentence from the proposition it expresses then the terms "truth" and "necessity" apply to the proposition expressed by a sentence, while the terms "*a priori*" and "*a posteriori*" are sentence relative. Given that it is true that Cicero is Tully (and whatever we need about what the relevant sentences express) "Cicero is Cicero" and "Cicero is Tully" express the same proposition. And the *proposition* is necessarily true. But looking at the proposition through the lens of the *sentence* "Cicero is Cicero" the proposition can be

seen *a priori* to be true, but through "Cicero is Tully" one may need an *a posteriori* investigation.

3. "The Meaning o£ 'Meaning,'" pp. 230 and 231.
4. For one alternative to my assumption see Monte Cook, "If 'Cat' Is a Rigid Designator, What Does It Designate?" *Philosophical Studies*, 37, no. 1 (January 1980). If Cook is correct much of what I say is wrong. I believe I can counter him, but to do so requires more than I can put into a footnote.
5. Hintikka, Moravcsik, and Suppes, eds., *Approaches to Natural Language*, pp. 518–31.
6. "Identity and Necessity," p. 160.
7. Ibid., p. 154.
8. "The Meaning of 'Meaning,'" pp. 238–39.
9. Ibid., p. 239.
10. For the sake of simplicity I am pretending that isotopes are distinguished by their isotope numbers alone. To accord with atomic theory as we know it I need a combination of atomic number and isotope number. This would complicate the telling of the Twin-Earth story, but the same point would emerge.

SUBJECT INDEX

AUTHOR INDEX